SHORT HEADS
AND TALL TALES

SHORT HEADS AND AND TALL TALES

Lester Piggott
with Roy David

Illustrations by John Ireland

STANLEY PAUL
London Melbourne Auckland Johannesburg

Short Heads and Tall Tales

Stanley Paul & Co. Ltd

An imprint of Century Hutchinson Ltd

62–65 Chandos Place, London WC2N 4NW

Century Hutchinson Australia (Pty) Ltd
PO Box 496, 16–22 Church Street, Hawthorn, Melbourne, Victoria 3122, Australia

Century Hutchinson New Zealand Limited
PO Box 40–086, Glenfield, Auckland 10, New Zealand

Century Hutchinson South Africa (Pty) Ltd
PO Box 337, Bergvlei 2012, South Africa

First published 1986
© Lester Piggott 1986

Set in Century Schoolbook by Tradespools Ltd, Frome

Printed and bound in Great Britain by Butler and Tanner Ltd, Frome and London

ISBN 0 09 166260 5

CONTENTS

*In memory of
Warren Sandman*

INTRODUCTION

Racing would be dull without its lighter side, the laughs that cushion the disappointments of a tough sport. In all my years in the game I have had a lot of fun along the way, and here I would like to share some of those moments with you.

I want to thank Roy David for putting together this collection of anecdotes, repartee and humorous stories which, I hope, will provide some pleasure as well as an insight into the Sport of Kings. Thanks also to John Ireland for his excellent cartoons.

CHAPTER ONE
THE RIDING GAME

Most people who follow racing will know that my father, Keith, was a well-known jump jockey of his time and later a successful National Hunt trainer who sent out Ayala to win the Grand National for a long-time family friend, 'Teasie Weasie' Raymond. His father, Ernie, was a great horseman and won the National three times – if you count the 1918 Gatwick substitute event, which he won on Poethlyn.

When you look at the statistics, my grandfather's achievements were quite remarkable, for his two Aintree winners, Jerry M in 1912 and Poethlyn in 1919, both carried topweight of 12–7 and Poethlyn was the shortest priced favourite ever to win the race – at 11–4. But to show how your luck varies in this game – he came down at the very first fence in the 1920 race, again on Poethlyn who was the 3–1 favourite.

I rode at Aintree on the Flat and even rode Red Rum to victory in a seller there when he was a two-year-old. However, I'm not sure whether I would have liked to have tackled those fences – hurdles were good fun and I managed to ride twenty winners over the smaller obstacles.

One statistic regarding Aintree no one has picked up is that four generations of the Piggotts have now ridden at Liverpool. If people start scratching their heads trying to think of the other Piggott, well – it was my eldest daughter, Maureen. True, she didn't ride in a competitive race, but a few years ago she did ride over half a dozen of the National fences with Richard Pitman and the amateur Ernie Fenwick when the BBC were filming a special preview of the race. Maureen is a successful three-day event rider in her own right and although she enjoyed the Aintree experience tremendously, I think she'll stick to what she knows best.

My grandfather's eldest brother, Charles, was a trainer. He set up an establishment at Cleeve Lodge, Cheltenham, after the First World War, and had a nice touch of luck with one of his earliest successes, a horse called Vaulx. Charles had served with the 3rd Battalion, The Worcester Regiment, and was engaged in that terrible fighting on the Somme. The village where he saw most of the action was a tiny place called Vaulx-Vraucourt – hence the name of his horse.

Vaulx won Cheltenham's National Hunt Handicap Chase in 1922 and 1924 and the following year, ridden by my father, landed the Welsh Grand National. But the best part of the story is that good old Vaulx cost Charles the princely sum of just £10 as a yearling.

My father often used to relate the story about the old-time jockey who was a very good rider but who liked a bet and consequently would sometimes 'pull' a horse if he'd had a bet on another. One day he was going to ride a horse that the connections fancied very strongly. As he said afterwards, 'The owners got this ridiculous idea before the race that I was going to pull their horse up, so they greased the reins. I just had to win after that, didn't I?'

An Irish trainer earlier this century woke on the morning of the National to find a snowstorm raging. Although there was a doubt about the event going ahead, quick as a flash he sent his lad into the village to buy several pounds of butter from the grocer's shop. The stewards inspected the course and, despite the covering of snow in patches around the track, decided not to cancel.

The trainer rubbed the butter into his horse's hooves so that the snow wouldn't ball under its feet. The trick worked and the horse won – a marvellous piece of ingenuity.

The Grand National riding story that tickles me most is when Bruce Hobbs became the youngest man to win the race at the age of seventeen, in 1938 when I was a mere two-year-old.

His mount, Battleship, was only a pony – 15.2 hands to be exact – but was a great jumper and had won two American equivalents to the National before coming over here to race. The Aintree fences then were even stiffer than they are today (they were modified after the Second World War), so much so that the drop on the landing side was much steeper.

Bruce and Battleship had coped tremendously well with what must have seemed very daunting fences – especially to this little horse who was still an entire and his young jockey. But at Becher's Brook the second time around

Battleship landed much too steeply and poor Bruce was heading for the side door. Then, just like the fairytale knight, the late Fred Rimell, who was aboard a horse called Provocative, came to Bruce's rescue – and hauled him back into the plate by his breeches.

There's no doubt that, but for Fred, Bruce was a goner. Instead he and Battleship galloped on to win the race while poor old Fred came to grief a couple of fences later on.

Although Fred was a top NH rider of his time, he never did win the National as a jockey. But he more than made up for that as a trainer and saddled the winner of the race a record four times, the last occasion being another winner for former hairdresser 'Teasie Weasie' with Rag Trade, who beat Red Rum in 1976.

I've ridden some right characters in my time – horses who had different idiosyncracies which I had to look out for and humour. St Paddy was one of them. I used to ride him at work on Newmarket Heath and he bolted on several occasions, once when a bird flew up beside him. He would just zoom off and it would be two or three furlongs before I could pull him up. I found it was best to keep him on the bridle, let him pull rather than let him off the bit, because he then became unsettled and wouldn't race.

Habitat was another good horse, very fast, but he landed me in it during the St James's Palace Stakes at Royal Ascot in 1969 and I ended up with a seven-day suspension.

The problem was that Habitat was rather fond of trying to bite other horses – he'd had a nibble or two at other runners at Haydock when I rode him there. This day at Ascot, Geoff Lewis was riding Right Tack and I think Geoff had decided to leave his challenge until the very last moment. As Right Tack loomed upsides us, Habitat swerved left in one movement and went to bite Geoff's horse. Habitat obviously didn't like any other horse to come past him when he thought he was winning the race – I've ridden several horses like that.

The incident happened so fast there was little I could do to stop him – other than pulling him up, and I probably would have been in even bigger trouble if I'd have done that. So I got seven days which I thought was most unfair.

Then, to make matters worse, Geoff got my ride on the Duke of Devonshire's Park Top because of my suspension – and he won the Hardwicke Stakes two days later.

The memory of Sir Ivor is very dear to me and I recall several people asking me before the 2,000 Guineas if there was anything that could beat me. A fall – that was all that was standing in our way. Before I had ever sat on him Vincent O'Brien had told me he was a 'hell of a horse' and it only took that first race on him – the Grand Criterium, France's top race for two-year-olds – for me to agree that Vincent sure was right.

Then there was The Minstrel, who was excitable and who tended to worry a bit. So before the Derby Vincent decided that we would put cotton wool in his ears to help deaden the noise from the Epsom crowd. When we got to the start I had to take the stuff out – it did the trick perfectly.

We'd all miss another jockey if he was suspended or injured and off the course for a while. Everyone was sick when poor Willie Carson had that terrible accident on Silken Knot in the Yorkshire Oaks a few years back. When someone like Willie goes missing from the riding scene it leaves quite a gap – he's always clowning about and there's hardly a dull moment in the dressing room.

I was riding in that race and got a glimpse of the accident. The filly broke a leg and Willie was sent crashing to the floor while the rest of the field trampled over him, knocking him about like a puppet. Even though he was in a bad way with a fractured skull, broken vertebrae and a fractured wrist, he was laughing and joking when I went to see him in York Hospital. After only a couple of days he was watching racing on the television and his guv'nor, Dick Hern, hit the nail on the head after he'd been to pay a visit: 'They had to plaster him all the way from his armpit to his wrist to stop him waving his arm about when he was watching the races on television.'

I know just what it's like – you can't help yourself riding the winner out at the finish from the hospital bed!

Willie was a week in the York Hospital before being transferred nearer home and he had so many visitors that the doctors put a ban on them. You know Willie, he was entertaining them all so much despite his obvious discomfort that his doctor said it was wearing him out.

One of the visitors was Geoffrey Summers, secretary of the Jockey's Association. He arrived at Willie's bed looking as if he'd just been in the wars. 'Hey nurse,' Willie shouted from his bed, 'you've got the wrong man in here.' Well it wasn't quite that way, but Geoffrey had tripped over in the car park on his way in and fallen on his face.

Of course Greville Starkey then tried to get in on the act. He must have been feeling a bit out of it so he decided to go and see Willie as well – only Greville was in a wheelchair. The day after Willie's accident Greville was injured when his horse dived under the front of the stalls.

He ended up with two very painfully bruised legs and was out of action for a week. And the name of the horse that crocked old Greville? Laugh a Minute!

Like all jockeys I've had my share of injuries, though all the spills could have been much worse. I broke my leg and my collarbone in a heavy fall at Lingfield early in my career and I've broken my nose three times as well as having had my share of stitches here and there. All in all, I reckon I've been fairly lucky. I'm not superstitious – but someone must have been looking after me.

One of the worst fears is that one day you might be dragged along with your foot stuck in the horse's stirrup. It happened to me a couple of times but, as a whole, I always used to put the fear of serious injury right out of my mind.

In 1970, just before a big-race weekend when I was due to ride in the Irish Derby on the Saturday and in the Grand Prix de Paris the following day, I had fractured a small bone in my foot after having been thrown from a horse on the Wednesday. As usual before such a big event there was a lot of media activity – Liam Ward was riding Nijinsky this time and I was riding Meadowville.

I had to go and see a bone specialist. He said I must take it easy although I would be all right to ride and he gave me a pair of crutches to take the weight off the damaged bone. I hobbled out of the surgeon's room only to discover that there was a posse of pressmen and photographers waiting around the corner. It required some quick thinking because I obviously didn't want a picture of me in the papers on crutches the day before the Irish Derby – so I flung the crutches down a manhole just in time.

The weekend didn't turn out too badly either, because I was second to Nijinsky on Meadowville and I won the Grand Prix de Paris on a horse called Roll of Honour.

There was also the affair when Windsor Boy got out underneath the starting stalls at Epsom early in the 1981 season – with me still on his back. You wouldn't think it was possible to get a horse and a man through that little gap at the bottom of the stall but we managed it. What worried me most as I lay there with blood pouring from my half-torn ear was that I had broken my back – the pain was excruciating and I thought I was finished with race-riding for good.

Poor old Windsor Boy went berserk and careered down the course before crashing into the rails, injuring a woman spectator, and then killing himself.

I also lay there thinking about my saddle being torn to shreds – they cost £100 each and the damn thing ended up in ribbons.

After a forty-five-minute operation on his damaged ear, which required thirty-one stitches, Lester surprised the racing world by declaring that he would be riding Fairy Footsteps in the 1,000 Guineas – just one week after the accident.

'It's no wonder they call him the iron man of racing,' said his surgeon Patrick Whitfield who was the consultant plastic surgeon at Roehampton's St Mary's Hospital. 'Lester was lucky not to have broken his back.'

For Mr Whitfield, the chance to operate on Lester was a way of saying thank you – 'I've won a good few bob backing Lester's horses over the years. Now I'll be having a fiver on him when he rides Fairy Footsteps,' he said.

Sure enough, the Iron Man was back in the plate, bruises and all, and not only duly won the 1,000 Guineas, but rode another five winners by the end of the meeting. The day after Fairy Footsteps's triumph, Lester was reading his newspaper and, to his amusement, saw a caption underneath a picture of the filly stating: 'Fairy Footsteps wins the 1,000 Guineas at Newbury.' He looked up and said with a grin: 'I told everyone she was a very good filly. She must be – to start off at Newbury and win at Newmarket!'

The ups and downs of racing were never better manifested than by Lester's experiences in 1977. Just three days after riding Robert Sangster's The Minstrel to win the Derby, Lester was aboard the same owner's Durtal who was the heavily-backed favourite for the Oaks. Sadly, however, the filly never even got past the post.

Durtal was jittery in the paddock and despite Lester's attempts to calm her she bolted on the way to the start. At the same time Lester's saddle slipped and he came off – narrowly missing the harrowing experience of having his foot caught up in the stirrup – and Durtal collided with the rails, hurting herself so that she had to be withdrawn.

Three weeks later Lester rode The Minstrel again, this time winning the Irish Derby at The Curragh. But less than an hour after that victory he was dodging death once more when one of his irons snapped at the start of a six-furlong sprint.

With his mount, Glencoe Lights, almost bolting, Lester fought desperately to keep the filly on the verge of control for the whole six furlongs until they passed the winning post and Lester collapsed from the horse in agony and from sheer exhaustion.

'That was a nightmare ride and he is very lucky to have escaped unscathed. It could have been a very nasty accident indeed,' said an Irish Turf Club steward afterwards.

Three Irish doctors quizzing him after the fall back in the first aid room were not sure whether to allow Lester to ride again that afternoon. 'You look rather shaken to us,' they said. 'I'm always shaken when I have ten grand on,' came the quick reply.

Even in the weighing room a little later, Lester was still feeling a trifle unsettled and an ambulanceman advised him to lie down for a while and give himself time to recover. 'Don't be daft,' Lester told him, 'I need my £14 riding fee in the next.'

Mike Watt was Lester's commercial manager. The bustling New Zealander is now boss of an international sports and personal management agency that includes some of the very best 'high-profile' names in the business. His daily schedule would be enough to grind mere mortals into the ground.

The commercial exploitation of a jockey might seem a simple enough task: after all, these are world-famous sportsmen, stars in their own right in a glamorous, big-money game. Unlike other sports, however, a personal endorsement of a jockey's kit hardly has its makers jumping up and down in excitement. The Borgs, Beckers and McEnroes of this world can sit back and watch the dollars pour in and so can the golfers, footballers and racing drivers as they put their name to the fast-selling consumer goods in the High Street. A Lester Piggott whip, saddle or pair of riding boots is hardly going to have little Johnny or Jane tugging at Mummy's hand to part with the pennies. So Mike has had to look to other areas – such as television advertising, paintings, prints, objets d'art and limited edition porcelain. And there have been occasions where he has had to turn manufacturers down – for head-scarves, for instance, and for animal rugs for cats and dogs – where he thought the familiar face might look rather inappropriate!

But Mike's 'laughs with Lester' haven't always been confined to the commercial side of the business. Like the first time he met the maestro and Lester promised to ring him within a couple of days to discuss a certain matter. When Lester called, Mike was out; his wife Gay, who would sooner be anywhere than on a racecourse, answered the phone. The brief conversation went like this:

'Is Mike in?'

'No, I'm afraid he's out right now. Who is it calling?'

'Lester Piggott.'

'I see. I think the best time to catch him at home would be a Saturday afternoon.'

'Mmmm... okay, I'll try again. But I'm usually rather tied up Saturday afternoons.'

On the Piggotts and their cash, Lester's father, Keith, said: 'The Piggotts have always thought a lot about money and when they bet they expect to win. I remember losing on a horse trained by one of the family who had had a good punt – no one would speak to me for three weeks.'

There was pandemonium during a Windsor night meeting when Lester was dumped from the back of a colt when he was five lengths clear and heading for an easy win. He had made all the running on the 4–1 second favourite and was coasting to success when the horse ducked and unseated him. The confusion then arose because Lester was convinced the incident had happened after the winning post. But the photo-finish camera then broke down and the verdict was left to the judge, Graham Wemyss, who said that Lester had fallen off before the line. He gave the race to the favourite Tamerboy while Lester left the track with a sore thumb – and the 'winner' that got away.

When Lester rode Never Say Die at Epsom in 1954 at the age of eighteen to register his first Derby success, he was not a popular man with the small bookmakers despite the horse's price of 33–1 – which made him a shock winner. For up and down the country the 'Boy Wonder's' reputation was growing fast and he had already become the housewives' choice. Thousands of small punters had put their shillings and half-crowns on young Lester and they had been amply rewarded.

After the race the Press gathered round the shy young man. 'What are you going to do tonight, Lester – paint the town red?' came the question.

'No, I'm going home to cut the grass,' said Lester, which is exactly what he did.

Three years later his second Derby winner came along in the shape of Crepello. Lester had won the 2,000 guineas on him just a month before. This time Crepello was the 6–4 favourite and the horse won in a fast time by a length and a half from Ballymoss who was himself reckoned to have been capable of winning a Derby nine years out of ten.

Lester jumped down off the horse in the winner's enclosure and was met by the same question – with a reminder that he had gone home to cut the grass after the Never Say Die victory.

'I'd better do the same again tonight then,' said Lester. 'I haven't cut it since!'

The day Lester tried to hoodwink officials at Doncaster on the opening day of the 1981 St Leger meeting led to a most painful lesson – it cost him a £100 fine. After a hectic time racing at home and abroad, he arrived at Town Moor without his medical book. If he had simply reported the matter to the stewards he could have got away with a fine of £7. Instead he told one official he had shown it to the first. When they checked with each other and demanded to see the book, Lester was forced to own up.

And pay the extra £93... ouch!

Another even bigger slap in the wallet came during that lovely summer meeting at the French seaside town of Deauville in 1979. In the £29,000 Grand Prix de Deauville, Lester was riding African Hope and was battling it out with French jockey Alain Lequeux on Jeune Loup for second place. Lester had dropped his whip approaching the final furlong and, although both jockeys had no chance with the eventual three-length winner, First Prayer, it was nip-and-tuck for the second prize.

As the two horses drew close together, Lester reached out and took Lequeux's whip out of his hand, then gave his own horse a couple of back-handers, and just got into second place in front of Jeune Loup by a neck.

Lequeux was not amused and reported Lester's whip snatch to the stewards. The incident had the packed racecourse crowd in stitches but the officials took a dim view and dished out a twenty-day suspension. Lester's mount was relegated to third place and Jeune Loup was placed second.

The ban meant that Lester missed not only Ayr's Western meeting but

the whole of the St Leger meeting too – losing him thousands in likely percentage prize money.

A tongue-in-cheek Lester marched out of the steward's room and announced to waiting reporters: 'I thought he'd finished with it so I asked him for it – I did say thank you.'

History almost repeated itself in the 1986 season, although the two jockeys involved were Mark Birch and Tony Ives and the venue was England not France. And this time Tony was on a beaten horse and Mark, who had dropped his whip a furlong before, did ask perhaps a little more politely than Monsieur Piggott.

Mark's horse went on to win under the whip. 'I definitely wouldn't have won without it,' he said afterwards.

Arnie Robinson, one of the hard-working band of northern valets, looked after Lester for a good number of years whenever he was riding in the North. In between races on a hot day Arnie would nip out and return with a giant ice-cream cornet for Lester.

'I'd have to be sharp about it because the damn thing would soon start melting otherwise, and often the ice-cream stall was a good way from the jockeys' room. He couldn't drink tea in between races, as some of the others did, because of his weight – it can soon add a pound or two.'

It wasn't long before Arnie started being nicknamed 'Lester's ice-cream punter' by all the other jockeys, who often pulled his leg about it.

'Sometimes Lester would be riding with just a three-quarter-pound saddle – it was basically a thin piece of leather with stirrups and I often wondered how he used to control a horse on such a flimsy thing. I used to wonder where he got his strength from – there wasn't a spare ounce of flesh on his body. Of course, Lester never used to say a lot in the changing room, but the other riders knew he was the guv'nor. He'd come out with those dry one-liners occasionally and have everybody in tucks.

'In the earlier days there was no racecourse commentary – they weren't allowed. But we always knew when Lester hit the front because we could hear them shouting from the stands while we were getting the tack ready for the next race. If a horse came home in absolute silence then you knew it wasn't one of Lester's!'

The avid punter was in no doubt where his priorities lay: 'I pay more attention to Piggott's bottom than I do to Brigitte Bardot's.'

CHAPTER TWO
OWNERS AND TRAINERS

Henry Cecil and I had a great partnership, one that helped me win the Jockeys' Championship title in 1981 and again in the following year. He is extremely dedicated and someone who I am sure will stay at the top for a long time to come. There aren't many races in Britain he hasn't won, but when it comes to racing in France, Henry will be the first to admit that he has never fared too well – in fact I think he's jinxed over there. Not that he has that many runners abroad – he's a home bird really and there's nothing he likes better than tending his roses at Warren Place.

The Grand Prix de Saint-Cloud in the July of 1974 was Henry at his French best. He had a horse in his yard called Relay Race, on which I'd won at Newmarket in May. Then we won the Hardwicke at Royal Ascot, so there was a fair amount of optimism that the horse would go well in Paris. In the parade ring I found that Henry had put the number cloth on the horse in the English way – over the weight cloth, which is the wrong way in France. As we were trying to resaddle Relay Race he got a bit upset, whipped round a couple of times, and shed his two hind racing plates. This naturally affected him during the race and he finished at the back of the field.

When I got back to where the horse was to be unsaddled I told Henry that he couldn't put a saddle between the two humps of a camel, though I put it more colourfully. Relay Race's owner, Sir Reginald Macdonald-Buchanan, was standing nearby. He hadn't heard what I had said to Henry – he was a bit hard of hearing – but Henry's wife Julie had. 'What was Piggott saying?' Sir Reginald said, hoping I had given him some sort of explanation for the horse's poor performance. 'Oh,' answered Julie, 'he just said the horse didn't run very well.'

Julie is Sir Noel Murless's daughter. I had eleven very successful years with Noel. He was a master of his profession and his record speaks for itself – nineteen Classic winners in a career that lasted over forty years. Although Noel rarely had a bet, he just couldn't resist the temptation one day when a bookmaker friend of his turned up at Warren Place. I don't know whether it was anything to do with Noel's brand of Scotch but the bookie offered 66–1 about Crepello completing the 2,000 Guineas – Derby double. Noel took the odds to £100, which was a small fortune in 1957 – almost enough to pay my cigar bill for a whole year. I always thought the horse never really showed his best because of his poor legs, but what he did show was quite good enough and Noel won a packet.

The bookie friend, seeing Noel not long afterwards, congratulated him on the big win. Perhaps Noel felt he was in the groove because he impulsively asked the chap to lay him £50 on the Queen's runner in the Oaks, Carrozza, at 100–8, which he did. Carrozza was only a pony, a bit lazy perhaps, but very brave. The race was one of those desperately close finishes that I relished (especially when I won). It seemed like we had to wait for ages for the result of the photo between my horse and the Irish filly Silken Glider, but in the end we got the verdict. And once more, Noel picked up his winnings – I think he stopped betting after that! He certainly didn't pass on the Midas touch to me when a few years later my wife Susan was expecting our first child and we were staying up for the Chester May meeting at the Grosvenor. I was so confident about our having a boy that I had a bet on it – one of those crisp fivers. And what happened? Maureen.

Another Oaks victory that gave me tremendous pleasure was in 1975 on Juliette Marny, trained by Jeremy Tree. Jeremy had two fillies in the race and it was touch and go whether I rode Juliette Marny or her stable companion, Brilliantine. In fact I think the racecard that day showed me riding both. These decisions aren't so easy as you might think, and I've got them wrong in my time. Brilliantine was the better fancied but when I got to the course and saw that the going was firm I started leaning towards Juliette Marny. I asked Jeremy what he thought. 'Don't ask me – it's up to you,' he said. He was right, it was up to me and I'm glad he didn't try to put me off Juliette Marny. I thought she would handle the ground much better than Brilliantine and that the blinkers she was wearing for the first time would help her concentrate. As it happens, I was proved right. Greville Starkey rode Brilliantine and she hated the ground and trailed in eleventh of the twelve. Juliette Marny skated home by four lengths.

Now that I'm training I'll have to cope with all those problems that as a jockey I could leave to someone else. Noel Murless used to tell a story about a bunch of two-year-olds he was working one summer when Sir Gordon was riding for him. It was before the Epsom summer meeting and, as each lot worked worse than the last, they returned to the house feeling very down-hearted.

'This might cheer us up,' said Noel, opening a bottle of champagne.

By the second bottle the two-year-olds were sharpening up no end and after the third there were some animals among them who were really quite something. During the fourth bottle Gordon was standing on the arms of his chair, singing but well forward with plans for next year's Classics.

It was then that they decided they might get Herbert Blagrave to join the party (he was then training his own horses at Beckhampton). There was a fifth bottle of champers, then a sixth ....

Herbert had his private plane waiting nearby to fly him down to Shoreham; he often stayed there for the Epsom meetings and his wife was down there waiting for him to arrive. When he and Gordon finally appeared, Gordon unluckily fell out of the plane onto his head. He got a real rollicking. But he still rode a treble the following day.

Ian Balding once had a different sort of problem assessing his two-year-olds. In the autumn of 1969 he had taken delivery of a very nice yearling and when the two-year-old began half-speed work the following March, the whole stable started getting quite excited. As Ian said, they realized that 'this fellow was either pretty good or the others were useless'. They were right on target. 'This fellow' was Mill Reef. The others were ... useless!

One of the things I never cared for when I was riding was if a trainer started giving me a long list of all the things I should do in a race. It reminded me of a quote I read about once which came from an American jockey who came to ride over here in the 1920s. On his very first ride the trainer began the tirade of do's and don'ts and was still going on when the jockey turned to him and said: 'Say mister, a good jockey don't need no orders, and a bad jockey can't carry them out anyway. So, mister, I guess you better not give me no orders.'

One of the Henry Cecil owners and a friend of Lester's was the ebullient Souren Vanian, an Armenian gentleman of extra large proportions with a capacity for enjoying himself almost in relation to his massive frame. He tended to provoke good-humoured jokes from his friends in racing. It was he who developed the Derisley Wood Stud at Newmarket, which housed such good horses as Glint of Gold, Posse and Siberian Express.

One winter Lester had been away riding for most of the off-season in Hong Kong and the Far East and got back home to Newmarket eager to catch up on the local news.

It just so happened that there had been a murder in the town that winter and now police were investigating the discovery of a large pool of blood outside the gates of Mr Vanian's stud. Someone told Lester about it. He immediately came up with the answer: 'I expect Vanian's cut his finger.'

Robert Sangster, the man responsible for revolutionizing the face of the international bloodstock industry during the past decade, recounts one of Lester's favourite devilish trick of 'borrowing' things ... like his car, his driver – even his helicopter.

'Lester is a great prankster and takes a lot of fun out of impish behaviour. He's not malicious or anything but sometimes the consequences can be damn annoying to people – which only makes Lester laugh all the more and in the end you have to laugh yourself.

'He always used to pinch Vincent O'Brien's *Sporting Life* and *Sporting Chronicle*. Vincent would go hairless and curse him but Lester would come out with some sort of a quip that would have everyone in stitches.

'His great trick was to use my car and driver who were waiting for me to leave a meeting. I think he did this twice to me, once in Paris and another time in Deauville. Lester had finished riding and wanted to get away from the track so he found out which was my car, walked up to the driver and flung his gear into the back saying: "Mr Sangster isn't coming back."

'By the time I came to leave I couldn't even see my car – of course it had disappeared with Lester. No doubt he was sitting in the back seat smoking one of his cigars and laughing his head off as the car took him back to his hotel or to the airport.

'At Phoenix Park, when Lester won the Phoenix Champion Stakes on Commanche Run, I had arrived by helicopter. As the afternoon wore on Lester must have thought he wanted to be off, so he went up to my pilot and in the most serious of voices, with a face to match, he told him that I

was staying in Ireland for the night – or something similar. When I went to the take-off point I had to phone up to find out why my helicopter had disappeared.'

Robert Sangster can also smile at another incident involving Lester.

'During a meeting at Goodwood I was flying to Deauville that evening from Shoreham and Lester was coming with me. I told him he must be at Shoreham by six o'clock so he arranged a helicopter to take him from the racetrack to meet up with me. Nick Robinson had asked if he could come over with me – he was with three of his friends – and, as that would have made up the six seats on the plane, I told him that was fine.

'They were also at Goodwood and asked Lester for a lift to Shoreham in his helicopter. I'm not sure whether Nick and his friends were expecting a free ride in Lester's helicopter but I would have thought that was most unlikely. Anyway when the 'chopper landed at Shoreham only Lester was in it.

'He strolled up to my plane lugging his saddle, with his blue-tinted sunglasses and stone face. When I asked where Nick and his friends were, he simply said: "They're not coming – let's go."

'I thought this was strange because Nick had definitely said they were coming so I decided to wait a few minutes. Then, at the edge of the airfield, I spotted this car doing about 100m.p.h. – yes, it was Nick and his pals who in the end had decided to drive down.

'I turned round to Lester and there he was with that impish grin on his face. I'm sure he would have loved to have taken off without them and to have seen their expressions when they arrived at Deauville by an ordinary scheduled flight. That's his sense of humour – it's on a grand scale!'

Vincent O'Brien is the greatest trainer in the world. That's not a unique statement of course, and one with which the record books would agree. Vincent's view on Lester was that he never said very much, but when he did 'it usually paid to listen.' So when Lester made one of his frequent visits to Tipperary to ride work at Ballydoyle on the two-year-old Nijinsky, Vincent was most anxious to hear Lester's opinion. It was the colt's first serious work-out and Vincent himself had great hopes of him. He greeted Lester after the gallop and waited for the all-important words. 'He'll do,' said Lester. Only two words maybe, but all that Vincent needed.

Another aspect of Lester's work-riding always infuriated the Irishman – although these days it brings a laugh or two and a shake of the head. Lester would 'do his own thing' on the gallops to see just how good a horse was and then, when he pulled up and trotted back to where Vincent was slowly simmering, he'd just smile and say: 'I'm sorry about that!'

The 1977 Derby success of Robert Sangster's The Minstrel was the signal to the racing world that the Sangster–O'Brien partnership had arrived in a big way. It would never have happened had the Aga Khan not turned down Lester's bid to ride the favourite Blushing Groom. Lester persuaded Robert and Vincent that it was worth The Minstrel taking his chance and so history was made.

A few days before the race Robert and the Aga agreed that win or lose they would have a thrash on Derby night at the fashionable London nightspot of Annabel's in Berkeley Square. According to an exclusive in the next day's *Daily Mail*, Lester had slipped away from Epsom, driven straight home and for dinner that night had eaten a frugal salad before going to bed early. Not so, however. Lester went along to Annabel's and joined the party in the club's private dining room. He tucked into two helpings of caviar, helped himself to a large portion of lamb, and rounded it off with a pudding before dancing and laughing into the small hours.

Who said Lester never enjoyed himself?

Charles St George – or to give him his full name of Charles Anthony Barbato (hence the CAB number plate on his Mercedes) – has been a friend and close associate of Lester for more than thirty years. The former Coldstream Guards officer, now a Lloyds underwriter, has owned such good horses as Primera, Lorenzaccio, the 1972 Oaks winner Ginevra, the 1975 St Leger winner Bruni, Giacometti, and Cellini, and was one of the syndicate owning the 1973 Arc winner Rheingold. More recently there was the mighty Ardross.

In all his years as a top owner he has been one of Lester's devoted allies and the maestro has repaid the loyalty many times over with his big-race successes in the black and white chevron colours.

One of Vincent O'Brien's promising horses in the early seventies was Apalachee. As a two-year-old Apalachee had impressed all who saw him at Ballydoyle, but it was August 1973 before the public got a glimpse of the Round Table colt, and even then it was in Ireland. The sight of Lester sitting tight as Apalachee carried him towards the winning post at The Curragh was all that his connections had hoped – especially when Lester turned and gave a long disdainful look at the opposition. Someone afterwards suggested that the judge had left his spectacles at home – the six lengths was more like ten.

It was no surprise that Apalachee started at 7–1 on for his next outing the following month, the Moy Stakes, again at The Curragh. This time the victory was a five-length margin despite conceding seven pounds to his opponents.

So for his third and final race of his two-year-old career the Observer Gold Cup at Doncaster was chosen. It was a race which, if he won, would put him among the winter favourites for the 2,000 Guineas and probably the Derby, for on his breeding he was bound to get the Epsom trip.

The big race was being televised but was being run early in order to accommodate a live football match being covered later in the afternoon's sports programme. Lester had arranged a plane to take him and Charles up to Doncaster and they set off in plenty of time. But, as Charles takes up the story, it was one of those days when things did not exactly go to plan.

'To start with it was a typical Lester plane – one engine! We set off and everything was going smoothly until we got near Doncaster. We couldn't believe it when we saw it was very misty with extremely low cloud and the pilot turned to us and said it was so bad that we couldn't land.

'Now Lester is a daredevil when it comes to situations like that and I'm sure that if he was in charge of the controls he would have swept down through the clouds and landed up the home straight – anything so he wouldn't miss his race. However, the pilot wasn't having any of it.

'Lester kept shouting: "Look at the time, you can land there." All that sort of thing. At one point he shouted that he could see the running rail through the cloud. In the end the pilot got so fed up that he turned round and said to Lester most forcibly: "I am the captain of this ship and you'll do as I say."

'Lester was most put out. "I thought it was a f – aeroplane," he shouted back at the pilot.

'Anyway he decided to land at York and the pilot radioed for a taxi to meet us there. I was getting worried myself when we finally landed because time was running out and Lester would have sprouted wings and flown to Doncaster himself if he could. We jumped out of the plane and ran towards the taxi with Lester carrying his gear in his usual bag. The taxi driver was rather old I'm afraid and I think Lester's mouth dropped when he saw him. Lester asked him how long it would take to get to Doncaster and when the old boy replied it would take much longer than we anticipated Lester got so despondent that he threw his bag at the poor chap.

'Fortunately for us, I spotted two police motorcycles and asked them if they could help us out. They were marvellous and we had a police escort all the way to Doncaster racecourse with our old taxi man driving down the A1 like Stirling Moss. We made it in the end – but what a nerve-racking experience.'

The race was a well-contested affair and Apalachee covered himself with glory, beating the French runner Mississippian, who had earlier won the Grand Criterium, by two lengths, with the third horse Alpine Nephew a further ten lengths away. Lester rode the perfect race, as usual, totally unflustered by the pre-race commotion which had almost cost him a winning ride in one of the best two-year-old races of the season.

Unfortunately, as is the way of racing, Apalachee never took his chance at Epsom, for which he was made winter favourite, and after running third to Nonoalco and Charles's other horse, Giacometti, in the Guineas, the colt was retired to Gainesway Farm Stud in Kentucky.

Lester was once invited to a Buckingham Palace reception. The Queen chatted to Lester and talk got round to the forthcoming St Leger. 'Would you be kind enough to ride my horse in the race?' she inquired. 'Well I don't know about that, we'll have to see,' Lester replied.

Someone tackled him a little later and asked him why he hadn't been a little more receptive to the Queen's idea.

'Because I fancy Athens Wood,' he said.

And Athens Wood he rode – and won.

Lester has often said that if he had not become a jockey, he would have ended up driving fast cars – on the motor-racing circuit. Lester's driving of fast cars on ordinary roads has been well catalogued and in 1977, after collecting his fourth endorsement for speeding in seven months, he was forced to hire a chauffeur. There was one occasion when he blamed a policeman for the size of his feet – having just run over one of them. Perhaps Noel Murless had the last word on Lester's driving: 'He drives a car like he rides a horse – if he sees a gap, he goes for it.'

Sir Noel had been worried that Lester seemed to be having a battle with several French jockeys every time he rode against them. At Ascot, a week after a French jockey complained he had been hit with a whip at Chantilly, Lester saw the trainer talking to the Queen.

Lester waited until they had finished their conversation before moving closer, just in time for Her Majesty to wish Lester good luck before she walked away. As Lester was getting the leg up his curiosity got the better of him.

'What did she say?' he asked.

'She said to stop b—ing about with those French jockeys.'

Lester replied, with a completely straight face, 'All right – I won't touch them this week.'

A trainer sought Lester's advice about a horse who had a habit of continually hanging to the left.

'The best thing you can do is to put a bit of lead in his right ear to act as a counterbalance,' Lester told him.

The trainer looked startled. 'But how the hell can I do that?'

Lester told him. 'With a shotgun.'

In 1960 Fulke Johnson Houghton became the youngest trainer around – at the age of twenty he took over the Woodway Stables in Blewbury, Berkshire, from his mother Helen. It was also the year when Lester became Champion Jockey for the first time with 170 winners when he was twenty-four years old.

Fulke and Lester were travelling to Worcester, which was then staging Flat meetings as well as National Hunt. They were in Lester's car, a portable 'sweat-box' in those days when Lester would wear two or three sets of clothing and drive on a sunny day with the heater on at full blast. On this occasion, Fulke remembered 'the car was better than any sauna and I was sitting there suffering, boiling hot and practically down to my underpants. Lester pulled into this pub car park, jumped out and said I wouldn't have time for a drink because he was only going to be thirty seconds. I was left gasping and it was twenty minutes before he came out! I told him I could have been in there enjoying a nice cold drink. "Too bad," said Lester. So I told him that I'd make sure his saddle fell off in the race.

'He must have taken my threat seriously. When it was time to saddle my runner, he handed the saddle to his father and said: "You'd better saddle this for me, Dad. I don't trust the b—!"'

Another time Fulke was driving Lester home after racing at Kempton when they passed an ice-cream seller – one of those tricycles with the

'Stop me and buy one' slogan, which was rather coarsely parodied in the sixties (with reference to precautionary goods) as 'Buy me and stop one'. It was a very hot day and just after they passed it Lester told Fulke to stop the car. He jumped out and came back with four cornets.

'Thanks, Lester,' Fulke said, holding out his hand.

'Keep off,' said Lester. 'You can buy your own if you want one.'

Then there was the time they were in America together when Lester was riding Ribocco for Fulke in the Washington International. During their stay there was a big reception at the French Embassy. 'We arrived there to see that couples were making a rather grand entrance by walking down this splendid flight of stairs and then being introduced to the assembled guests by a footman at the bottom of the stairs. It was all very elegant and just like you've seen it at the movies, a tradition from a bygone age. But there was no chance of an elegant entrance from Mr Piggott and myself. Lester took one look at the proceedings and, as we were half-way down the staircase, he turned to me and said: "Shall we hold hands?"'

Fulke's mother, Helen Johnson Houghton, the twin of Fulke Walwyn, suffered the day a young Lester received a special present for winning on one of Sir Victor Sassoon's horses. At least, Jimmy Lindley swears the story is true. As most racing fans know, Jimmy is one of Lester's greatest admirers, as well as a friend, and is always entertaining BBC viewers with his quips about 'the man 'isself'. Jimmy tells the tale thus: 'Sir Victor had this rather large car, a Ford Continental, that Lester very much had his eye on. So one day Lester was due to ride one of Sir Victor's horses and asked if he could have the car as a present if he won. Sir Victor agreed and, after Lester duly won, he sent the car down to where Lester was living.

'Well, Lester was chuffed, but what he didn't realize was that the damn thing only did about ten miles to the gallon. Anyway he thought he would take it out for a spin so he rang up Fulke and told him: "You've given me a lot of lifts so I'd like to take you out in the car – and bring your mother along too." Lester arrived at Blewbury, Fulke and Helen got in and off they set for a nice tour of the countryside. After about ten minutes Lester pulled up at a filling station, jumped out and started to fill up with petrol. The car had two tanks, one on each side, and must have taken, oh, let's say about forty gallons in each tank. The total bill came to about eighty quid.

'Then Lester turned to Helen all helpless and said: "I've come out without any money!" Poor Helen had to cough up. I think she's still waiting for Lester's cheque.'

The former Upper Lambourn trainer Ben Leigh engaged Lester to ride one of his horses at Kempton. Going out of the parade ring the horse started playing up and dumped Lester once, then again, and once more out on the track.

In the race itself the animal did not do so well and the combination were not in the frame, much to Leigh's annoyance. He came rushing up to Lester after the race and told him: 'That's the last time you ever ride for me.'

The poker-faced Lester, who'd had enough of the horse, turned round and said: 'Well it looks as though I'll be out of business then.'

Yorkshire owner Percy Raine of Maunby near Thirsk and his trainer David Barron had a dream come true when Lester agreed to ride Percy's home-bred Miss Import. It had been both men's ambition to have Lester in the saddle before he finally retired, so they were both delighted when he agreed to ride the mare in a decent five-furlong handicap at York. Although the five-year-old had won four times the previous year, that season she had so far run four times without success – but had shown she was returning to form on her previous outing at Haydock.

In the parade ring David had just two words for Lester as he gave him the leg up: 'Help yourself,' he said. And that was exactly what Lester did, keeping the mare handy until going on and winning by a clever three-quarters of a length. Said David: 'It would never have entered my head to have begun to tell him how to ride the mare – he probably found out more than I knew just cantering her to the start.'

Two weeks later at Ascot was a repeat performance. 'Please yourself,' David told him before dashing off to the stands to watch Lester bring Miss Import home by three lengths, leading from the start in the Rous Memorial Handicap. After each race David had two more words for Lester: 'Bloody brilliant.'

It was Steve Cauthen's first season riding in Britain. During the 2.30 race at Kempton The Kid pipped Lester at the post aboard a three-year-old trained by Barry Hills. As he unsaddled and walked towards the weighing room, Lester was looking rather nonplussed. But at least he had an explanation. 'Three or four times inside the final furlong the winner tried to bite me. It's that Barry Hills. He thinks of everything.'

Lester was once asked how long it would take him to set up as a trainer, considering all the organization, premises, horses and the hundred and one other aspects of a new job to be arranged. 'About five minutes,' he replied.

Charles St George actually advised Lester not to take up training. 'Why try to start all over again? I advised him to pack it all up and be a senior citizen. They say that I am Lester's financial adviser but they don't know Lester — he wouldn't take advice from the Governor of the Bank of England.'

Those magnificent men in their flying machines who ferry jockeys, trainers and owners all over the country might end up on occasions having to repeat Bruce Forsyth's famous words, 'I'm in charge', but there was one day when Lester had to come to a pilot's rescue — by acting as navigator.

This time Charles had hired the aircraft, which was taking him from Elstree to Doncaster but stopping at Cambridge on the way to pick up Lester.

'I had with me an owner friend — four foot six inches tall and very nervous of flying. I assured him everything would be all right — and of course they were the famous last words. On our way to pick up Lester we seemed to be taking a long time and we eventually reached Cambridge very much overdue. The trouble was, as the pilot told us on our way, that the plane's compass wasn't working. When we told Lester what was wrong he ignored the pilot's protestations that the plane would have to be grounded, jumped into the co-pilot's seat and declared: "I know the way — just follow the railway line."

'That was just what the pilot did and under Lester's expert eye we landed at Doncaster in one piece though I'm not sure whether my pal was too happy with the arrangements. We had a good afternoon's racing and met up at the plane again for the return journey.

'I was sitting in the back with my pal on my left and Lester was in the co-pilot's seat again. I don't know what happened but when I looked out of the window all I could see below us was water. I thought to myself "What the hell's going on?" — I could see us ending up in France or somewhere. It transpired that we were over the Wash but the pilot thought he had better turn back and land at the first aerodrome he found and that was just what he did.

'We landed among all these Delta bombers and other military aircraft and the next minute the plane was surrounded by Military Police. By this time my pal had become rather emotional and started explaining his rights as a law-abiding citizen. Lester was telling them who he was, I was trying to convince them that we were not interested in their Delta bombers, our pilot was telling them about his broken compass – it was straight out of a Brian Rix farce. And all this time there was a wing commander who had driven out in his jeep telling us that on no account must our plane be moved.

'My pal felt the need to go and spend a penny and I'm sure that as a law-abiding citizen he had every right to use an RAF lavatory under the circumstances. As he was being marched off in between two very burly MPs, Lester watched until they had all gone out of sight. He then turned to me and with a most serious expression asked: "Do you think we'll ever see him again? Maybe they'll shoot him."

'That was pure Lester. After a while the wing commander arranged for a mechanic to fix the plane, my pal returned safely, and we took off once more. It was while we were in the air that our pilot, who was Australian, informed us that he had only arrived in Britain the day before and was sorry about all the inconvenience. That just about put the top hat on it all. When we finally landed back at base, Lester jumped out and said to me: "That's some pilot – and he won't be getting paid for this!"'

Throughout their long association Charles has always been amazed by Lester's great courage and his coolness, especially under pressure. Lester used to stay with Charles at his London home, usually on the eve of a big race, and on the eve of the Derby one year Lester was relaxing in the convivial company when the telephone rang. It was a call for Lester. 'Yeah... yeah,' they heard him say, completely impassively, then 'Right-oh, goodbye.' He replaced the receiver and returned to join in the conversation.

It was only some time later that Charles asked him who the caller had been. 'Oh,' Lester replied, 'it was just someone who said I was going to be shot tomorrow.'

There was another time when both Lester and Susan were staying with Charles before a big race. During the night Susan burst into Charles's room calling out 'Come quick, I think Lester's dying.' Charles rushed into their room to find Lester rolling on the floor in agony. There was nothing he could do but summon a doctor immediately.

In due course the doctor arrived and delivered his verdict: poor Lester had a kidney-stone and there was absolutely no chance of his riding the next day. 'For one thing,' said the doctor, 'there's a good chance that he'll fall off the horse. I'm afraid my advice is that he does not ride.'

After the pain subsided a little, Lester had a verdict of his own: 'Bloody doctors, they don't know anything!' He ignored the doctor's advice and went out and rode the next day without telling anyone else about his night of agony.

A couple of days later, and while the Piggotts were still guests of Charles and his wife, Lester took his kidney-stone complaint into his own hands, so to speak. Not long after dinner he disappeared into a bathroom to emerge several minutes later with the cause of the whole trouble captured for posterity – in Mrs St George's silver tea-strainer. She was slightly put out at Lester's choice of receptacle, but she had to admire such a classic case of do-it-yourself.

Lester had been involved in a particularly bad accident during a race in France when he had been knocked out cold. As he had been riding a Murless horse, one of the first people to see him as he lay in a Paris hospital was Lady Murless.

True to form, the very first thing he asked for when he regained consciousness was... his wallet. Soon afterwards Charles went to see his friend who was being kept in for a couple of days, mainly for observation but also because he was having trouble with the vision in his right eye.

Charles recalls: 'While I was sitting at the side of his bed a nurse came up with this yellow pill. Lester took it off her and was just about to swallow it when the nurse started shouting and gesticulating wildly. You know what the French are like – the damn thing was a suppository.

'Lester was most upset. He'd swallowed the last two.'

One of the most successful owners from the middle fifties until he retired from racing at the end of the seventies was the television and radio rentals king David Robinson. A mysterious character who shunned publicity, he was most particular about finalizing his horses' running plans himself and this led him to change trainers quite frequently. His one Classic victory, Our Babu in the 1955 2,000 Guineas, does not reflect the great success in lesser but still important events and on several occasions he topped 100 winners in a season. In the early seventies he was the owner of something like 160 horses, in the care of his private trainers Michael Jarvis and Paul Davey.

One day when Lester was due to ride a fancied Robinson runner, the owner was not amused to learn that his jockey had an injured foot. There was a slight contretemps outside the weighing room as Piggott emerged in the famous green and red colours.

'You're not riding this horse if you've got a broken foot,' said Robinson icily.

Lester countered: 'I've got thousands of bones in this foot – and only two of them are broken.'

Needless to say, he went out and rode yet another winner.

A partner with Charles St George in the Rheingold syndicate was Henry Zeisel, in whose name and colours the Barry Hills-trained colt ran. Apart from being a most enthusiastic owner, Henry had been an officer in the Austrian cavalry and knew a thing or two about horses. He was also a gifted musician and had played the violin in the Viennese Philharmonic Orchestra. Before Rheingold's success in the 1973 Prix de l'Arc de Triomphe, Lester was asked if there was a particular present he would like if he won.

'Tell Mr Zeisel I'll have his fiddle,' came the reply.

Now Lester might not know the difference between an A-string and a G-string, but his tongue-in-cheek reply was certainly not out of tune. Henry's 'fiddle' was a priceless Stradivarius.

The likeable Brough Scott, whose live-wire personality and excitability in front of the television cameras does not do justice to his talents as a gifted racing columnist and writer, was almost on the receiving end of the Piggott punching power the day he confronted Lester with a question many thought was below the belt.

Lester was being interviewed before millions of Channel Four viewers at Epsom during the Spring meeting of the 1985 season when the news came through that Walter Swinburn had been given a suspension for his 'careless' riding of Lord Grundy in the previous race. This meant that Walter would unfortunately lose the ride on Shadeed who was most people's idea of a likely winner of the 2,000 Guineas in just over a week's time.

Brough immediately seized the news and put Lester right on the spot by confronting him with the question: 'Will you now ride Shadeed in the Guineas, Lester?'

Now Lester might have stepped into 'dead men's shoes' in the past but not while they were still warm and the question caught him absolutely off guard. It was also highly unlikely he was going to announce his decision in public just seconds after Walter's ban was announced. Shadeed's owner Sheikh Mohammed and his trainer needed to be considered first anyway and the decision was up to them to say nothing of the connections of Lester's intended mount, Bairn.

However, Brough persisted with the line of questioning and got away with it. Lester clearly decided to pull his punches and simply began to fiddle with his socks – as if pulling them up – in embarrassment.

One of Brough Scott's endearing features is that he is not immune to sending himself up. He recalls when he deputized for Sheikh Mohammed in the parade ring at Arlington Park, Chicago, as owner of the Lester Piggott-ridden Noalto in the Budweiser Million.

It was an honour to be representing the absent Sheikh in such an important event. And here was Lester, smiling and flicking his whip against the top of his riding boot as he weaved his way through the parade ring and approached Brough, Noalto's owner.

But what do you say to a jockey who's seen it all before a thousand times? What sort of instructions could you possibly give? So instead of giving a serious lecture on tactics, Brough meekly asked: 'What are your plans, Lester?'

Lester gave him a long hard look, then pointed to the far side of the course. 'See those starting stalls? Well, after them it's one and a half circuits of the track.'

When Slip Anchor, in the apricot colours of Lord Howard de Walden, flashed past the winning post in the Epsom Derby of 1985, with the nearest pursuer a further eight lengths away, that jovial and most sporting owner had the biggest thrill of his racing life. Born in 1912, Lord Howard de Walden has been Senior Steward of the Jockey Club three times and is one of racing's administrators who loves to see the lighter side of a sport that often takes itself too seriously.

Two incidents with Lester which particularly amused Lord Howard de Walden also show the vagaries of ownership in the Sport of Kings. One of his trainers in his early days was Jack Waugh, with whom he continued to have horses until Jack's retirement in 1970 from Newmarket's Heath House Stables (subsequently bought by Sir Mark Prescott). Jack trained some good horses for his lordship including the filly Sanlinea, third in the 1950 St Leger, Amerigo, who won the 1957 Coventry Stakes, and Ostrya, winner of the Ribblesdale Stakes six years later. It was with a lesser-known animal that Lester teamed up to ride at the old Alexandra Palace track more commonly known as 'Ally Pally'.

'Jack couldn't go racing that day but we spoke before I left for the racecourse and he firmly told me to tell Lester that the horse must not be subjected to a hard race and that the animal was to be given every chance. In the parade ring I passed on these comments to Lester and went off to watch the race. Well, Lester is Lester – he jumped off smartly, made all the running and came home alone. What could one say to Lester after that? And all he said to me as he went to weigh in was: "That was easy."

'Exactly the opposite happened when he was riding Fool's Mate one day at Newbury for me. Fool's Mate was a dear favourite of mine and he gave me a lot of pleasure and on this occasion he was lumbered with top weight. Well, Lester jumped off in front, tried to make all the running, but was swallowed up and faded in the final furlong to finish down the field. I caught up with Lester as he was unsaddling the horse and he just raised his eyes heavenwards and exclaimed: "That was a damn silly way to ride the horse." For once I had to agree that he was right.'

The following poem might strike a note of recognition from those in the training fraternity. It comes via former trainer Rosie Lomax, author unknown:

THE TRAINER

'I envy the life of a trainer'
Said a chap that I met on a plane.
'A lucrative life in the open
Surrounded by birds and
champagne!'

'High living at Ascot and
Deauville
At several times of the year,
Then home for a healthy old
gallop,
Why, it's life at ten thousand a
year!'

Amazed at the stranger's
delusions,
At a loss if to laugh or to cry,
I wondered if I should correct him
And thought it at least worth a
try.

The 'open'! My God, have you tried
it
In winter with snow on the
ground?
At seven o'clock in the morning,
And more wrinkles than inches
around.'

Our social life may seem all roses
But the birds aren't for us, and the
'Fizz'
You use for reviving an owner
When he finds out how bad his
horse is!

Peers, prostitutes, pansies and
punters,
Does that sound a pretty odd
bunch?
On the turf they are prominent
owners
And we have the whole boiling to
lunch!

You'd get quite a new view of
Ascot
In tails, a top hat on your head,
Sprinting uphill to the paddock
With a saddle and two stone of
lead!

Deauville has many attractions,
Your owners adore them of course
They go out to dinner with Pollett
And you go home minus your
horse.

Your Head Man awaits your
arrival
With relish he tells you his news
The Travelling Man's broke his
leg, Sir
The Box Driver's gone on the
booze.

Bert's had a row at his digs, Sir
The new girl is pregnant of course
Sir Harry is coming round stables
There's ringworm all over his
horse.

The wages are up thirty bob, Sir
And I'm going down with the 'flu.
You thank him and try to look
cheerful
Goddammit what are you to do?

The telephone never stops ringing
It's Sunday but you'll get no rest
The owners consider it their day
For getting complaints off their
chest.

Then there're jockeys, those
Knights of the Pigskin
A look at their Ladies will tell
For your winners they get all the
credit
And most of the presents as well!

The betting boys bunch as at
Christmas,
By day they're extremely polite,
But spend all their spare time
conspiring
To get at your horses at night.

The Press have the last word in all
things
As Trainers they'd all top the tree
The fact that they haven't a
licence
Is terribly handy for me.

The Stewards demand
explanations,
But listen with cynical looks,
It's obvious in their estimation
That trainers are all licensed
crooks.

It's wonderful how we continue,
In spite of complaints from our
banks,
To render such service to racing,
For peanuts and damned little
thanks!

It's normal in other professions,
To prosper, retire and die,
But trainers go on training horses
I'm buggered if I can think why!

CHAPTER THREE
JOCKEYS

I was eighteen when I finally realized that the world can be a cruel place. It was after that well-documented ban following the King George VI of 1954 and the Never Say Die fiasco when I was stood down for the rest of the season and forced to move to Jack Jarvis's yard at Newmarket for what amounted to 'correctional training'. It was a fat lot of good because Jack was ill in bed and I hardly ever saw him for most of the time. In the end the ban lasted more than three months.

Those were the days when the old-school jockeys still had racing in their grip. Although, as now, jockeys were not allowed to bet, a lot of them did – they even had a bookie's runner who was in and out of the jocks' room all afternoon. Sometimes they even ended up beating a horse they'd backed.

There were no starting stalls then and I remember one starter who would line up the field at the tapes – and not let them off until he had asked Gordon Richards if he was ready or not. If Gordon gave him the nod then he'd let the field go no matter what anyone else was doing.

Racing's always been full of characters and Gordon was one of them. I remember the racing writer and author Tim Fitzgeorge-Parker telling me about the day his editor on the Daily Mail *got into a lather when the news broke that Gordon had been taken into hospital.*

The editor asked Tim if he had Gordon's obituary already written but when Tim finally made contact with the man himself, the ailment turned out to be far from fatal.

Gordon told him: 'Same old thing. Wet saddles – piles.'

One of the hardest things about Epsom on Derby day is... getting there. The whole world and his dog seem to converge on the track and unless people set off very early in their cars there's just no guarantee they'll get there by the start of the first race. In latter years I always travelled by helicopter, driving into London by car, then catching the 'chopper from the London heliport. But in 1983, the year I rode Teenoso to win, I very nearly didn't get there on time at all.

I left home in good time and we were all set to take off in the helicopter when a racegoer's topper was blown off his head and got tangled up in the rotor blades. We were delayed for over half an hour.

All sorts of things happen when you have to travel. Mind you, it is something you get used to and most of the leading jockeys these days think nothing of riding in America on a Sunday. We'd leave after racing Saturday, ride in a big race in the States and then come down to earth by riding at a bread and butter meeting like Leicester, Warwick or Windsor. There's all sorts of talk about jet lag and the like but we seemed to cope all right. Four of us rode in the Arlington Million in Chicago one weekend in the August of 1983 – the year Pat Eddery won the race on Luca Cumani's Tolomeo. When we got back here, I rode a four-timer at Epsom, Steve Cauthen got a treble at Newcastle and Pat notched up a double at Warwick.

Pat must have earned something like £40,000 as his share of Tolomeo's first prize at Arlington Park – and just over a ton for the Warwick double!

They say that Epsom is a very tricky course to ride but I wouldn't know – I never used to look. Every track has its own idiosyncracies and one thing about Epsom is the matting they have covering the two roads which run across the course. Normally it wasn't too bad, because once they put grass over the mats you wouldn't know they are there. There was one particular day though when the wind was blowing like anything and most of the grass had blown away. As the field approached, Geoff Lewis, who was riding a horse called Spanish Prince, must have wished he had a parachute with him. The horse took one look at the mat and tried to jump it. We were going at full speed and it had been a long time since Geoff had ridden over jumps. The last I saw of him was when he was twenty feet or more in the air – and still rising.

Lots of jockeys like to play squash, work out in the gym, or play tennis or football during the close season to keep themselves fit. I always used to watch my weight, ride abroad, and then gradually get back to full fitness just before the start of each season by riding plenty of work. There was one season, however, when I fancied a spot of running. I don't know what got into me really but I ended up running so much that when the season did start and I went to put on my special lightweight riding boots the damn things wouldn't fit because my calf muscles were bulging so much.

Willie Shoemaker is a good friend and we have both had some memorable times riding against each other over the years. Bill is five years older than me, is just four foot eleven tall, wears size two shoes and weighs about six and a half stone wet through. But his strength in the saddle is tremendous and he's a brilliant horseman – no wonder he's ridden more than 8,000 winners in his career.

Jeremy Hindley is a successful Newmarket trainer and his wife, Sally, does a lot of work for charity, and she organized a match where Bill and I would ride against each other and the £10,000 prize put up by Long John Whisky would go to the Multiple Sclerosis Society. I was riding Spanish Pool while Bill drew Princes Gate and I think the bookies made me a shade odds-on with Bill at 5–4. Princes Gate won the race and it was one time I didn't really mind losing because the whole day was for such a good cause. I think Bill also won the Bonusprint Stakes that afternoon as well, then dashed off to board Concorde and fly off home – where he was riding in the one and a half million dollar Louisiana Derby the next day.

Bill's visit and our match had attracted a lot of publicity and we tried to accommodate everyone who wanted pictures and stories and television and radio interviews. But there was one national newspaper who wanted the pair of us to dress up in seventeenth-century gear and fight out an imaginary duel for the cameras using rapiers. It didn't take us long to consider the idea and reject it – about five seconds. I wasn't going to look a nancy for anyone. Bill was also most reluctant:

'They would have needed a mighty small shirt,' he said, 'otherwise it would have looked as if I was wearing a nightie.'

Steve Cauthen rode his 800th British winner half-way through the 1986 Flat season, but it doesn't seem all that long ago since he came over here as a fresh-faced young man to start riding for Barry Hills. I like the quote about Steve that Affirmed's trainer made after Steve had ridden the horse to win the US Triple Crown in 1978.

He said: 'They say Steve is eighteen and comes from the bluegrass country but I don't believe them – he's a hundred and three and comes from another planet.'

Apart from the likes of Sir Cecil Boyd-Rochfort, Sir Gordon Richards and Sir Noel Murless, there haven't been that many knights of the turf – except for the day when about a dozen jockeys had this honour bestowed upon them.

Unfortunately Her Majesty knew nothing about it and it was Willie Carson who performed the duty. It was at the end of the 1978 season when Willie had just won the championship title with a total of 182 winners. He had also won the Wilkinson Sword Jockeys' Association championship, which netted him a cheque for £1,000 and just over double that amount for the Injured Jockeys' Fund. On the last day of the season at Doncaster Willie received his trophy which turned out to be a Wilkinson sword. So what did he do when he got back to the dressing room with it? He proceeded to 'knight' all the other jockeys in the place... 'Arise Sir Joe, arise Sir Pat, arise Sir Greville!'

I know that Harry Wragg used to think a lot of the riding skills of Brownie Carslake, the Australian who rode with great success over here between the wars. Carslake was very strong in a finish and Harry used to say: 'I never used to know where that so and so was hiding.' People said he could 'lift' horses over the line – a lot of his wins were by the minimum distance – and it seemed as though he put everything into those last few strides. It made me chuckle because I've read the same thing about myself... 'Piggott literally carried the horse over the line.'

That's why I hope you'll share the laugh with John Ireland's splendid cartoon on the front cover of this book. I'll tell you what though – my back didn't half hurt after a while!

Lester was riding at his favourite northern track, York, at one of the big meetings and was in tremendous form, with several winners already under his belt. There is always a great rivalry between the North and the South at such times – particularly among trainers and jockeys.

One northern-based rider who had seen all the major prizes being lifted by the southern big boys thought that, at last, he was on to a winner. During the race his horse was going really well and at the distance he kicked on and left the field standing – surely this one *was* going to win easily, he thought.

Inside the final furlong he heard what all jockeys hate in such circumstances – the sound of galloping hooves coming upsides. Out came the big stick, but his horse had given all and the jockey knew it. There was only one thing for it: he would have to give the challenging horse a crack over the head in the hope that the stewards would not notice, or, if they did, that he could claim it was accidental.

He turned round, raised his stick, and was met by the awesome sight of Lester sitting as still as a mouse with the proverbial double handful – reproachfully shaking his head as if to say 'Don't you dare!'

He didn't and Lester collected again.

Brent Thomson is a good jockey and a nice guy. He came to ride in Britain in the May of 1984 having ridden almost 1,000 winners in Australia where he was stable jockey to champion trainer Colin Hayes. It didn't take him long to get established with a retainer to ride the Robert Sangster horses and one of his golden moments was when riding that owner's Gildoran to win the Ascot Gold Cup the following year. A lot of racing people were also impressed by his manners, his smart dress-sense and his good looks.

When Lester was in Australia in the close season following Brent's first year in Britain, he met Hayes who was keen to hear news of his protégé.

'Your boy's making a big impression in England,' said Lester.

'That's great news,' said Hayes. 'Is he going to be champ?'

'Oh yes,' Lester grinned, 'and I think he'll make it as a male model too.'

Julian Armfield, the compiler of the Jockeys' column in the Sporting Life since 1979 and racing correspondent of Thames Valley Radio, has come across some weird and wonderful stories in his time. But the one he likes most concerns the Irish jump jockey who rode with considerable success in the seventies and who gave his weighing room colleagues a great deal of merriment during his first few months in Britain.

As was to be expected, the young man quickly befriended his fellow ex-patriots Ron Barry and Jonjo O'Neill and whenever possible arranged to travel with them to the races 'until I find me bearings, then I'll be all right so I will.'

Big Ron and Jonjo arranged to meet their new-found friend on their way down to Kempton one Boxing Day for the King George meeting and agreed to meet him at the Charnock Richard service area on the M6 at 8 a.m. in order to give them plenty of time to drive south in case the

weather was bad. They arrived ten minutes earlier and ordered a drink at the coffee shop. By 8.15 when there was no sign of him they began to get worried and decided to comb the shop, transport café and other likely places but all without success. Another half an hour went by before Big Ron had a brainwave. 'You don't think...' he said turning to Jonjo who, at the same time, exclaimed: 'I bet he's still trying to find those bearings.'

Up they both got and, dashing over the bridge, arrived at the north-bound service area to find the intrepid hero sipping his second pot of tea: 'Morning fellas – what kept you?' he said.

Bruce Raymond, who quit Britain to ride in Hong Kong for the 1986 season, shakes his head in disbelief when he remembers the time he was returning to Newmarket after a day's racing. He was driving Lester's Mercedes while the man himself took a back seat.

They hit a fast stretch of road. 'Put your foot down, Bruce,' came the order from the back. Half a minute later the speedometer needle was pointing to the 130 m.p.h. mark and Bruce was beginning to perspire just a little.

The next thing, Lester leaned over and Bruce could feel him breathing down his neck. 'Come on, put your foot down,' Lester reiterated.

Bruce pointed out he was already doing a hundred and thirty.

'I know,' said Lester, 'but put your bloody foot down.'

Doug Smith was one of Britain's top jockeys in the forties, fifties and sixties. By the time he had retired in 1967, his tally included five Jockeys' Championships, two 2,000 Guineas (Our Babu, 1955 and Pall Mall, 1958) and two 1,000 Guineas (Hypericum, 1946 and Petite Etoile, 1959). He then went on to train the 1969 Oaks winner, Sleeping Partner.

He was one of many riders of the time who would pull Lester's leg about his reputation for meanness. Yet, as he admits today, Lester would be the first to help him out if he ever found himself in dire straits.

'It used to be a game with Lester. I'm sure he tried it on just to see how much he could get away with.'

One day he and Lester had flown to Lingfield and had booked a taxi to take them on to the racecourse. It was the same driver who had often ferried Lester to and from the track and he knew of Lester's passion for

ice-cream. So when Lester asked him to stop because he wanted to help himself to a large cornet, it wasn't too much of a surprise.

'Do you know, that Piggott never gives me a tip – not all the times I've driven him,' the driver said to Doug as Lester left the taxi. Then he added: 'After we get going again you'll see me look in the driving mirror. When I do, just brace yourself.'

Lester soon returned with two whopping cornets and proceeded to tuck into one of them. They hadn't gone more than a hundred yards when, sure enough, Doug saw the driver's eyes in the mirror and held on tight. The driver braked as hard as he could, plunging Lester's cornets straight into his face.

'Sorry about that, Mr Piggott,' the driver said. Doug could see he was delighted.

With televised races and the stewards' patrol camera there is not much that any keen-eyed steward need miss during a race (even though there may still be local stewards around who could do with the Jodrell Bank telescope). In the old days, however, quite a few incidents went unnoticed and unreported, mainly in the guise of what we would call today the 'professional foul'.

Lester is the first to admit that he was no angel – his will to win was often quite ruthless. In the hurly-burly of a race, jockeys need to look after themselves, dish out as good as they get.

Doug Smith laughs now at the day he got on the wrong side of a young Lester – eighteen years his junior. It was at Sandown in the early fifties and before the advent of crash helmets. Doug had already ridden two winners and was going for a treble on a fancied horse. Lester, on Doug's outside approaching the bend into the straight, had him boxed in.

'Keep in, keep in,' Lester shouted.

'I'm coming out,' Doug replied, gradually moving his mount out.

'No, you're not,' Lester told him.

To Doug's amazement, Lester then turned his whip over in his hand – and clocked Doug one over the head with the heavy end. In fact Doug did eventually move out and won the race, but on the long trot back to the winner's enclosure he was furious. He considered reporting the fact to the stewards, but by the time he got to the weighing room, he had changed his mind and decided he would accept an apology instead.

They had two dressing rooms at Sandown then, and Lester was in the opposite one to Doug. But they met face to face a few minutes later at the scales.

'Are you going to apologize, Lester?' Doug enquired.

'No, what for?' Lester replied.

By the evening Lester could have seen 'what for'. Poor Doug had a lump on his head which he describes today as 'bigger than any egg I've ever had for breakfast'. And he adds: 'Now you know just why jockeys had to start wearing skull caps!'

It is always the practice of one of the Big Four bookies' representatives to ask a couple of the riders in the first race exactly how the ground is riding. One day at York the ground was bottomless after several days of incessant rain and Lester, riding the short-priced favourite, was well and truly beaten.

After Lester unsaddled and was making his way back to the weighing room, the Ladbroke's representative rushed up: 'Is it treacherous, Lester?'

Lester took one look at him. 'Yes,' he replied, 'for the punters.'

Former royal jockey Harry Carr could be said to have owed his six Classic successes to a moderate horse called Impressive and a race at Hamilton Park worth £207. A leading jockey in India just before the Second World War, Harry returned to England after the conflict to find that, at the age of twenty-nine, his skills had quickly been forgotten. So he found himself with few rides and, by the middle of 1946, decided that if Impressive did not win then he would pack it all in and go back to India.

Impressive duly obliged, however, and Harry landed the job of first jockey to King George VI with Captain Cecil Boyd-Rochfort, riding over eighty winners by the end of 1947, his first season for the new connections.

Always with an eye for a practical joke, he decided at Brighton one day to try and play a trick on Lester. He took one of the orange-coloured plastic girths which go round an ordinary girth and help keep the saddle in place, filled it full of water and put it in a long box surrounded by straw. At first glance it could have been a salmon.

Grabbing a valet, Harry asked him to take the box into the weighing room and give it to Lester with his compliments. And to complete the deception he had written the words 'Fresh salmon – with care' on the outside of the box.

The 'salmon' was duly handed over, but the quick-thinking Lester changed his mind and asked his valet to put it 'in the boot of Mr Carr's Mercedes'. And it was only when Harry arrived home that night that he discovered the joke had backfired – the 'salmon' had leaked all over the boot of his brand new car.

A top jockey who shall remain nameless was once asked what he thought of Lester. This was what he said: 'Well, they all say that Lester is mean but it isn't true – he's twice as mean as they say. They say that he's difficult to get along with and that's not true either – he's impossible. They also say that he's a great jockey but that's certainly not true – he's the best the world will ever see and the word great doesn't do him justice.'

A favourite quip among the jockeys about Lester and the Scotsman Sandy Barclay concerns the day when both attended the christening of another jockey's baby daughter. Everything was going fine until Sandy caught sight of the collection plate coming round, piled high with fivers.

Sandy immediately fainted – and Lester carried him out.

They say that Lester has used his deafness in one ear to great advantage over the years – in other words he often only hears what he wants to hear. But Willie Carson says quite candidly: 'When Lester was on that telephone touting for rides there was absolutely nothing wrong with him. In fact he could teach us all a lesson – he was a master at it. Now I suppose he'll be just as effective booking the right jockey to ride his horses!'

Geoff Lewis, who had that wonderful partnership with Mill Reef, would dearly have loved to have beaten Lester in the race for the Jockeys' Championship. Although the former hotel page boy never won the title of top jockey, he was runner-up to Lester for two years running and won five Classic races, including the 1971 Derby on Mill Reef. Geoff's highest total of winners in a season came in 1969 when he accumulated 146 successes – seventeen fewer than Lester who took the crown.

The two were neck and neck in the title race and Geoff looked as though he might take the lead with four rides at Hamilton Park, two of them fancied Henry Cecil runners. Lester got to work on the telephone.

He phoned Henry a couple of days before the meeting and told him: 'Geoff will be at Nottingham that day, so I'll ride your two.' Henry duly informed the Press Association who send out advance riding arrangements and these were published the day before the meeting in the *Sporting Life*.

Seeing Lester's name down to ride the two Cecil mounts, Geoff immediately got on the phone and Henry told him: 'But Lester said you'd be riding at Nottingham so I've given him the rides.' 'The cheeky so and so,' roared Geoff, 'that's a jump meeting.'

In the end Lester did ride the horses and won on them both. Geoff today still laughs about it, though 'I don't think I would have been laughing if there had only been a couple of wins between us at the end of that season.'

Geoff remembers those days as being tough – more so because to beat Lester for the title was not only one of his biggest ambitions, but winning the Jockeys' Championship while Lester was still riding was the hardest job in racing.

Says Geoff: 'Lester was the epitome of dedication. If he made up his mind about something then he'd go and do it – even if it meant travelling anywhere in the country to ride in a seller providing it had a good chance. To win the title when Lester wasn't around would have been okay, but to have beaten Lester to the punch would have been tremendous.'

Talking of 'to the punch', Geoff even lost out during a race at Sandown when there was a bit of argy-bargy between him and Lester after they had turned into the straight. The whips started flying and, to their consternation, they were spotted by the stewards. At a subsequent inquiry both came out of the stewards' room smarting at the fact they had just been fined £50 apiece.

'There was a bit of bumping,' says Geoff, 'and Lester hit me with his whip, so I hit him back. Afterwards as we were walking away I suggested that as he hit me first he should pay my fine. Lester just gave me one of those special laughs as if to say "You must be joking" and walked off chuckling to himself.'

Pat Eddery was in the changing room with Lester on a particularly hot day at Sandown and was just waiting for Lester to reach into his trouser pocket for some cash to send his valet out for an iced drink. At last his moment came and he gave Des Cullen the nod in a prearranged leg-pull.

Des had often paid for drinks for the lads but had noticed that Lester had never bought one back. So, eyeing Lester with the loose change in his hand, he piped up: 'I'd love an orange drink.' Lester didn't flinch, so again, but this time a little louder, so everyone in the room could hear, Des repeated: 'I'd just love an orange drink.'

Lester looked up, and said – much to Des's chagrin – 'I suppose I'm not really thirsty'; and put his money back in his pocket.

Jimmy Lindley recalls the night he couldn't believe Lester's generosity. 'Lester isn't as mean as they make out – he's much worse than that. But seriously, all the things he and Susan do for charity never get a mention. Where money's concerned though, Lester loves to have his own private jokes and that's how it was when a group of us were on our way back from the races and had decided to stop for dinner. As we pulled into the restaurant car park, Lester astonished everyone by announcing extremely boldly: "I'll pay for dinner tonight lads."

'We were all flabbergasted – but still chuffed. We all tucked in heartily and we were on to the coffee when the waiter brought the bill to the table. "Over here please," said Lester while we were all looking at each other and thinking this couldn't be true. Lester had a big cigar in his mouth and he reached to his back pocket and pulled out a big wad of notes, which he started counting out on to the plate while the waiter watched. "I'm afraid we can't take that here, sir," the waiter told him. It was a wad of that Shell "funny money".

"'It's all right," said Lester, "I've been abroad – you'll be able to change it at the bank."

'Needless to say, we all ended up paying for our own meals. But it was the night we nearly had a meal on Lester!'

Stories that Lester's love of money meant that he relished each crisp fiver like a rare jewel might be a little over the top but Joe Mercer recalls the day they were both travelling home from the races. Joe had only about five shillings on him while Lester had a roll of notes.

That didn't worry Lester: 'Get the ice-creams in, will you Joe,' he said, 'I haven't got any change.'

Another time, some twenty years ago when the pair were riding in Malaya, Joe ended up owing Lester money – two hundred dollars which he had borrowed.

'I wrote Lester a cheque but signed with it the fictitious name of Pierre André so he wouldn't be able to cash it. Then I popped it in an envelope and addressed it to Lester. Would you believe it – he only went round to the bank and talked them into cashing it. He nearly got us both locked up.'

American jockey Darrel McHargue was a victim of an owner wishing to prefer Lester's talents in a big race. He was replaced by Lester as partner for Commanche Run in the 1984 St Leger. Fair enough, Lester was a freelance and was hardly going to say no if an owner wanted to use his services. With all the games of musical chairs that accompany a big race, the freelance can often find himself without a ride at all. After all, it is the owner who owns the horse and pays the bills.

Lester went on to win on Commanche Run, riding a race only he could have ridden to beat the all-time record of Frank Buckle's twenty-seven Classic wins. On the morning of the race, after McHargue had publicly decreed that 'there should be a law against Lester Piggott' and 'I never want to race in England as long as he is around', it was pouring down. McHargue did not bother to go to Doncaster and had told everyone: 'I'm so fed up with it all that I won't be there – I'll be playing tennis instead.'

As Lester was arriving at the course he was asked if he thought the torrential rain would affect Commanche Run. 'No it won't,' he said with a cheeky smile, 'but it'll ruin McHargue's tennis.'

Lester's father, Keith Piggott, always told him to think not about how he won but how he lost. The philosophy might explain the lack of a Cheshire cat grin as he walked to the weighing room win after win: to win was almost automatic; losing often meant blaming himself.

One day, after winning a big race in which he rode brilliantly on a well-backed favourite, he walked towards the weighing room impervious to the delighted shouts from the punter behind him.

'Give them a smile, Lester,' said a bystander.

'Why should I? If I lost they'd only throw things at me,' he said.

The Australian jockey Bill Pyers rode for sixteen years in France landing there in 1964 from Melbourne where he was Champion Jockey eleven times. Bill often stayed with Lester when he was riding in England, just as Lester was a guest at Bill's home whenever he rode in France. And the pair were always playing tricks on one another.

Bill retired in 1980 with over 2,400 winners behind him and now lived on 'Millionaires' Row' in Lamorlaye near the famous Hôtel du Lys, an area next to Chantilly inhabited by many of France's famous horsemen. One of the tales Bill loves to tell is a marvellous piece of embroidery based on Lester's television appearance as the winning rider after his very first Derby success on Never Say Die.

'So Lester won the Derby and was all set to do the BBC television interview in the studio, for which he was being paid £100. In those days he used to speak far worse than he does now – he was very shy as a young man as well. Anyway, Lester arrives at the studio and they sent him over to make up. "'Ere, what's this?" he says. "I'm not having all this stuff on me for just £100 – you'll have to give me £200." So they agree to the new figure and the interview goes ahead. The interviewer asks Lester to tell the audience in his own words just how the race went but Lester mumbles away so badly that no one can understand a word he says. Afterwards there are numerous complaining telephone calls to the studio.

'About a week later a faith healer comes to town and is going to perform at Wembley Stadium before a huge crowd of 100,000 people. Now this affair is being televised and the viewers' choice of who should be healed goes to two people – Lester, and a footballer who is crippled for life and is on crutches.

'The big night arrives and the footballer hobbles up on the stage with Lester following and the faith healer tells them both to go behind a large curtain before he asks the people to pray. "Now I promise you that within a few minutes that footballer will be able to throw away his crutches and will soon be playing for England while you, Lester, will emerge with a voice like Mario Lanza," says the faith healer, giving Lester a microphone.

'The lights dim and the faith healer starts his prayers, which end with a crescendo of organ music. "Now throw away your crutches," the faith healer demands of the footballer. The crowd gasps in anticipation at the movement behind the curtains. "Now it's your turn, Lester," the faith healer shouts. "No more mumbling, say a few words to everyone in your new Mario Lanza voice."

'From behind the curtain comes exactly the same Lester voice as before: "He's fallen over!"'

Bill Pyers again. 'Whenever Lester came over to France we would always sit next to each other in the jockeys' room because Lester couldn't speak French and in those early days neither could I. One day Lester asked me if I would change him some money and handed me £100 in tenners with the outside tenner folded round the bundle – the way banks did it in those days and similar to how you might pick up your winnings from a British bookie. I gave Lester the going exchange rate in francs and, several days later, paid the money into my own French bank. Well, this happened several times, on each occasion for £100, and when I checked my bank statements I thought to myself: "These banks must be making a fortune at this rate of exchange." It was much lower than I was giving Lester.

'Another time it was £200 and then one weekend Lester asked me if I would do the honours again and handed over three wads of £100, each which I said I would change for him. That day we were riding at the old Le Tremblay track and as I had to go past Le Bourget Airport I thought I might get a better rate of exchange if I used the *bureau de change* there. Lester was with me when I went up to the cash desk and acted like I had just got off a plane and wanted the £300 changing into francs.

'The cashier started counting each wad and then re-counted them each time with a puzzled look on his face. It was only when I queried it that I found out just why I had been getting such a poor rate of exchange from my own bank all this time – there was only £90 in each wad and Lester had been helping himself to a tenner from each bundle before handing me the money. I turned round and there was Lester laughing his head off.

'Not long afterwards we were both riding at Maisons-Laffitte and Lester came and sat down beside me in the dressing room, put his hand in his bag and pulled out a box of fifty Havana cigars worth about £200. Then he tossed them into my lap without saying a word. "What's this then, Lester?" I said.

'He just looked at me and said: "You smoke, don't you?"

'So I suppose I got all my money back plus a very healthy interest.'

Lester's cousin, the former top jockey Bill Rickaby, recalls when he and Lester and several other jockeys had been riding in Scandinavia and had just touched down at Heathrow. Lester, who had won the big race, had been unable to resist buying several boxes of very good cigars but the customs officers must have spotted them a mile off because they nabbed him at the gate.

'These aren't mine – they belong to all these other passengers,' said Lester, tossing the precious cigars to anyone who would catch them.

After finally clearing the boys in black, the party was some distance from the car park and Bill was just about to board an airport bus when Lester tugged hold of his arm and suggested they should all get a cab.

In they climbed and three of the party, Bill included, asked to be dropped off at the car park. Lester, who was going on to the main terminal building, shouted: 'Hey lads, what about five bob each for the fare?'

Without thinking, they all coughed up and it was only as the cab started to pull away that Bill saw the cab's meter registering – just 2/6d.

The year was 1963, the date 9 November. The forty-nine-year-old grandfather Scobie Breasley, who had won a Jockeys' Championship the previous two seasons, was attempting the hat-trick. Lester Piggott, at twenty-eight, was attempting a follow-up to his first title success of 1960 when Scobie was the runner-up. The score was 174 to Lester and 176 to Scobie, with six races to go on the final day of the season and the last time racing would be held at Manchester's Castle Irwell track. There was a special Manchester November Handicap party at the city's Midland Hotel, with over 200 racing enthusiasts, owners, trainers and jockeys gathered for the celebrations.

Throughout the evening there was an atmosphere of almost black humour. Neither Lester nor Scobie got nearer to each other than thirty paces although, occasionally, each would sneak a quick look to see what the other was doing. It might have been 'Gunfight at the OK Corral'.

Precisely at ten-thirty Lester made his move – he went to bed. After a quick stroll in the night air, he went to his room leaving strict instructions that on no account must he be disturbed – 'unless the place is on fire.' Scobie still remembers the evening: 'I was laughing and joking with colleagues and friends but there was still this uncertainty inside me – after all, Lester and I had four rides the next day and anything could have happened. In the end Lester rode one winner and I didn't get one but I still won the title by the shortest of margins. I think Lester then decided that no one was going to beat him the following year and he was unstoppable after that – he went on to be Champion Jockey for the next eight seasons!'

Pat Eddery was once asked what he would do if he ever won a million pounds on the pools. 'I'd ring up Lester and ask him to invest it for me,' came the quick reply.

When Willie Carson was asked what he thought about Lester, the wee Scot replied: 'Lester's a lovely bloke. He is surrounded by this mystique and everyone wants to keep it that way.

'I could never compare my talent with his. Mine was not built in heaven – I had to work like a dog. I was simply one of those people who was in the right place at the right time.'

He couldn't have thought that about York in the October of the 1984 season when he was riding the Queen's Blakeney colt Rough Stones in a field of four. Wearing blinkers for the first time, Rough Stones was the even-money favourite. The stalls opened, the horse reared up, screwed round and trapped his head in the next stall. By the time Willie extricated the beast, the other three runners had already travelled half a furlong and all poor Willie could do was to trail in last, to the boos of the furious punters who had plunged on the royal runner. He hardly expected them to give him a free drink – but one of them did. He threw a whole pint of best bitter all over him.

Willie Carson was flat to the boards, his arms going in that unmistakable pumping style that has won him so many admirers as the man who never gives in. And the effort looked like paying off too, as his horse took the lead well inside the final furlong. Then up popped Lester to pip him on the line. 'I beat yer, I beat yer,' Lester shouted.

Willie couldn't resist the temptation as Lester's bottom sailed past him. He raised his whip to swipe the famous backside – but missed that as well. The stewards didn't though and they had Willie in for attempting to hit another jockey. It was only when he and Lester explained the situation that they took no further action... and the pair of them came out with their arms round each other's shoulders, still laughing.

Pat Eddery and Willie Carson always like to pull Lester's leg. They call him 'Leslie' Piggott, which stems from the day a rich business man new to racing misheard Lester's name during the introductions and referred to him all day as 'Leslie'.

During Lester's last season in the saddle the three jockeys went to ride at a Holsten invitation meeting in Hamburg. In the private jet on the way home a couple of bottles of champagne were cracked and soon everyone was in good spirits – you could say cruising nicely at 33,000 feet.

Pat and Willie suspected that it might be Lester's last season even though at that time no announcement had been made. Pat gave a wink to Willie, turned to Lester, who was sitting across the back seat of the aircraft, and shouted: 'Leslie, Leslie, have you sorted out your stable jockey for next season yet?'

Lester smiled and said nothing.

'I'll be your stable jockey. I'll be your number one, Leslie,' Pat continued while Willie chuckled that inimitable laugh.

'That's my job,' Willie rowed in.

'All right,' said Pat, 'we'll both ride for you, Leslie, how's that?'

'Yeah,' said Willie looking across at Steve Cauthen (who now travels by his own helicopter), 'you supply the helicopter and we'll sign up tomorrow, Leslie.'

'And the Rolls to take us from the landing strip,' roared Pat.

'And we want a fully stocked bar in the back,' added Willie.

And on, and on, they went until the rest of the party joined in – all at the expense of poor old 'Leslie' who had to sit and take the lot.

It wasn't long afterwards that Willie was overheard teasing Lester about his riding days coming to an end and the fact that he would start training – even though Lester had no such plans.

'Anyway, I'll ride for you Lester,' said Willie.

'No you won't – you'll be too bloody old by then,' came the reply.

Reg Hollinshead's stable jockey, Steve Perks, was one of several Northern riders who whittled away the time between races by playing cards in the changing room. It was a time when rummy was all the craze. Lester had just come in from riding a race when he spotted the game in progress.

'I'll join in,' he said, 'but make it pontoon.'

All the others round the table were taken aback because no one had seen Lester playing cards before and most of them thought he probably hadn't a clue how to play pontoon in the first place.

At first Lester wanted to borrow his stake money and the lads agreed to give him credit. After a while things were going fine and Lester was collecting on every round when the other players bust in their bid to reach 21. It was only after the fourth or fifth round that they discovered Lester was 'sticking' with cards totalling only 13 or 14 in his hand – contrary to the rules, which state you cannot stick with any number under 16.

Things then started to go badly and Lester was soon down on his luck. Then came a bumper kitty and all the players dropped out bar Steve and Lester. Everyone gathered round to see the finale – Lester was showing 17 while Steve, who was acting as banker, had 16.

'What do you want to do, Lester, stick or twist?' said Steve.

Lester rubbed his chin thoughtfully. 'Stick,' he mumbled a trifle unclearly. Steven wanted to 'twist' and turned over a four – Lester pounced on the opportunity. 'I said I'll twist,' said Lester grabbing the four out of Steve's hand. Steve, rather startled, had to turn over another card for himself – a 10, which meant he bust.

Lester won the game, counted his winnings and reckoned he had just broken even. 'That'll do me,' he said and walked out for the next race.

The late Harry Wragg, the 'Head Waiter', who with Sir Gordon Richards dominated racing in the 'thirties and 'forties, rode thirteen Classic winners. Not bad for a boy from a non-racing family who started his working life in a Sheffield flour mill. The story of how he mastered the art of riding racehorses is an object lesson to anyone who does not have the patience to persevere. After joining Robert Colling's Newmarket Bedford Lodge stable on a wage of a shilling a week, the young Yorkshireman was keen to start the business of riding as soon as possible and his big chance came when the head lad told him to ask the guv'nor to put him up on one of the horses at morning exercise.

Bold as brass, the young Harry took a deep breath and stepped forward with the request. Colling looked down sternly from his hack at the small youth: 'But tell me, boy, can you ride?' 'Not half, sir,' came Harry's reply. In truth the answer should have been 'Not a quarter, sir,' because all Harry did know was that you sat on the horse's back facing the head. Such technicalities as how to hold the reins, adjust the leathers or how to balance were mere trifles as he got the leg up next morning under the boss's watchful eye.

As the string moved out towards the Heath, it was taking Harry all his courage to stay aboard – and they had not yet moved out of a walk! Suddenly, one by one, the lads wheeled to the left and began to gallop up Long Hill. Harry sat there dumbfounded, the tears welling in his eyes as he watched them speeding off, the paddock sheets flapping away like birds in flight. He looked at the head lad: 'I can't do that,' he pleaded. 'Nonsense, follow me,' came the order. So off he set, bouncing up and down at first, then clinging on to the mane for dear life as his mount strode out at a fair clip. By some miracle he made it to the far end of the gallop despite finishing somewhere round the horse's belly, and all under the watchful eye of the guv'nor who sent two of the lads to escort him back to the stables in case he fell off. Before reaching the yard, one of the lead horses started playing up and lashed out, catching Harry on the side of the head. The next thing he knew he was in hospital with a fractured skull.

Now many a lad would have called it a day at this point. Seven days a week of hard graft and a clip round the ear if you were caught doing nothing would have sent all but the most determined back to the safe haven of a factory job. Not Harry though, even if he was now to spend five weeks in hospital – and without telling his father in case he was ordered home. When he eventually came out of the hospital he was immediately put back on a horse and asked to canter up the gallops. This he managed to do more or less in a similar fashion as before until his horse reached the end of the gallop and stopped abruptly sending Harry over its head – and on to his own. It wasn't the last time he ended on the deck either, but he tried and tried again, and slowly became proficient at what was now almost an obsession. After six months in the yard he was an up and coming young rider.

However, he was still filled with admiration at the tough guys in the stable, the older lads who could ride anything – or so they boasted. One day, Harry tried his luck riding an animal which had just arrived with a fearsome reputation. He was soon aboard the colt, only to be thrown ten feet into the air as soon as his bottom hit the saddle. A repeat bid ended with him twenty feet in the air. Harry strolled around the corner to find one of the toughest riders in the yard and told him what had happened but added that on the second occasion the horse had stood as quiet as a lamb. 'We'll soon sort this b— out,' said the rider marching forward to view the animal.

Thirty seconds later he was inside the paddock and had climbed aboard the brute, only to be thrown twice as high as Harry. 'Try him now, he'll be all right,' shouted the mischievous apprentice as the work rider picked himself up off the ground. And try again he did, another half a dozen times, until a crowd of lads had gathered round to see the antics of both horse and rider. Of course, there was nothing better than such a challenge to the other riders and the next one stepped forward determined to succeed where his pal had failed. By now the poor horse was visibly tiring but he still had enough energy to throw the new rider once before he got fed up and allowed himelf to be led back to the stables with his conqueror aboard.

It was only when they rounded the corner that the biggest surprise of all was discovered. For there was the previous owner of the horse staring in disbelief. 'Crikey, you lot work fast – the horse has never even had a piece of tack on his back before today, never mind a rider.'

CHAPTER FOUR
CUTTINGS AND JOTTINGS

Throughout all my years in the saddle I've had this sort of love-hate relationship with the media – I hate them to love me! It gets a bit much when they shower you with all those superlatives and the purple prose. If you believed everything they said you'd think I was superhuman. Mind you, I did like to tease them sometimes, especially when they started asking those daft questions. Strangely enough, I found that telling the truth often got the biggest laugh.

I remember after one big race when I'd pulled out all the stops. I knew the horse under me was out on its feet but I suppose the win did look easier from the stands than it actually was.

Afterwards, the reporters gathered round. I think someone thrust a microphone in front of my face and asked: 'Just when did you think that you'd won the race, Lester?' I looked at him for a moment or two, then simply told the truth: 'At the finishing post.' They all thought it was hilarious, yet it was the truthful answer.

During my final season the spotlight was on me even more than usual. They all wanted to know when I was retiring, the exact day, and so on. A journalist rang me one night for a chat and asked me if I did retire what was the one thing that I would miss most. I just had to tell him: 'Trainers telling me how far I'm going to win.'

Undeterred, he followed up with the question: 'Well what are you most looking forward to in your new career as a trainer?'

'Not much,' I told him. 'You see, I'm not really one of those people who gets excited about the future – I take it all in my stride.'

There was a great atmosphere at Nottingham on my final day as a jockey in Britain, in some ways rather a sad day for me. They printed a special souvenir racecard and I agreed to sign autographs. There were hundreds of people queuing up – the line stretched from the winner's enclosure to the paddock. They were all ages, men, women and children. One elderly gentleman, who had been waiting patiently for some time, got his turn and I signed the racecard for him. 'Do you know, I've been waiting over thirty-five years for this day,' he said. And I replied, 'So have I.'

Earlier there had been a press conference organized by the Nottingham Racecourse executive. One of the questions, no doubt the world was dying to hear, was: 'Lester, what do you think will be the biggest adjustment you'll have to make – in what area?'

Everyone went quiet while I had a think. Yes, I knew what would be the biggest adjustment – and where. 'I suppose I'll have to let my trousers out a couple of inches – around the waist.'

I was relieved to ride a winner from my five rides that day – the aptly named Full Choke for John Dunlop – and afterwards there was a ceremony in the parade ring where I was kindly presented with several mementoes. It was then that the well-known ITV broadcaster Derek Thompson burst into a rendition of 'For He's a Jolly Good Fellow' – in a singing voice that might not threaten Sinatra but would give a vocally ambitious cat a hell of a scare.

I rode nine Derby winners in my career and they all gave me a great thrill. Epsom on Derby day is a very special place with a magic all of its own – in fact the Derby meant more to me than any other race.

My first Derby winner, Never Say Die in 1954, was a memorable one. Then there was the splendid moment on Sir Ivor in 1968 and the marvellous Triple Crown triumph of Nijinsky two years later – a year when I also won the 1,000 Guineas on Humble Duty. The two that stand out in my mind, however, were the victories of Roberto in 1972 and The Minstrel in 1977 – both trained by Vincent O'Brien, as were Sir Ivor and Nijinsky. What pleased me was that both races were only won in really exciting nip and tuck finishes: even I didn't know who was the winner until virtually the last stride.

There is another Derby that I remember particularly vividly; and not because I won – in fact I just got pipped. It was on Gay Time in 1952, my second ride in the great race, and me just a lad of sixteen. I thought I had a good chance of winning but in the parade ring the horse spread a plate and had to be reshod. I could sense that this bothered him, and by the time the new racing plate was fitted all the other runners had gone down to the start.

Things didn't work out too well in the early stages – if you haven't got a good position by the time you hit Tattenham Corner you can kiss your chances of winning goodbye. On Gay Time I knew I was too far back reaching this point and I didn't get much of a run round. But once we straightened for home he started to pick up and all of a sudden I realized we had a good chance of winning. Unfortunately the Aga Khan's horse Tulyar proved too strong and we just couldn't peg him back. I got beaten three-quarters of a length. I tried not to show it but I felt terribly disappointed. I've sometimes thought of what might have been but for the horse pulling off that shoe.

When you're returning aboard the winner to that tiny enclosure reserved for the Derby winner it's a feeling that is hard to describe. I felt good after winning the 1983 Derby on Teenoso, who was trained by long-time family friend, Geoff Wragg. It was the year when the race was run on very soft ground but Teenoso was a very good horse and handled the heavy going really well.

I didn't have any real problems in the race and Teenoso won well enough, beating Carlingford Castle three lengths. It was after we had pulled up and were walking back on the course towards the winner's enclosure when there was an incident I've been reminded about since.

A photographer, I suppose trying to get the first picture, ran towards us and, on the soggy ground, tripped right in front of Teenoso. When you're sitting aboard a horse who has just won the greatest race in the world and is instantly worth several million pounds, the last thing you want is for something to upset the animal so that he might injure himself.

It had become the practice of ITV, who were televising the race all round the world, to send their man down on to the course with his microphone so he could get the first reaction of the connections as they were leading the horse in. On this particular day it was that man D. Thompson again, walking alongside us for his on-the-spot interview.

Of course, when this photographer fell, Teenoso shied and I had to catch hold of the reins. You can imagine that I wasn't very pleased and I told the fellow to go away in the strongest terms I know. But the microphone picked up my words – even today Derek still maintains that half the world heard what I said.

I can have a chuckle about it . . . now.

We all know that winners are hard to come by, no matter what you do in racing. A journalist told this true story some years ago and it shows to what lengths some punters will go in their search for success.

It happened at a large city bookmaker's shop one Saturday afternoon. An Irishman rushed into the shop with a £10 bet to win on a runner at The Curragh – it won at 5–2.

None of the Irish races were being covered by the 'blower' that day, but the manager thought there was no way the punter could have discovered the result so quickly even though in normal circumstances any pay-out is withheld until the Monday when the official 'off' times can be found in the *Sporting Life*.

As it was a relatively small sum to pay out, the manager duly handed the punter his winnings. Half an hour later, however, the same chap rushed in again, this time with a tenner on a 2–1 shot. That won too, and the manager paid up.

Then the lucky punter returned with a £5 to win on an outsider – it won at 50–1. The manager refused to pay but the punter claimed he had a case – which ostensibly he did – because he had been paid out on the previous two wins and, if they had lost, the shop would presumably have kept the losing stake money.

The manager gave in and started counting out the winnings. After all, he reckoned, how could the man have *known* the result?

But the plot was uncovered when a regular punter at the shop sidled up to the manager and told him he had just seen the Irishman huddled over a radio at the end of the street. And that afternoon there were four races being broadcast *live* from The Curragh.

The Irishman made a quick exit, never to be seen again. His version of The Sting had very nearly paid off.

Another similar fiddle happened when a gang – one of them a technician – delayed the commentary to the shop by thirty seconds. It gave them just enough time to pop around the corner and place their bet. But their greed was their undoing. For after two small winning bets, they upped their stake to £100. And when the manager tried to lay off the bet with another shop the manager there told him: 'You must be joking; the race is over.'

There are lots of similar tales where the bookies have got to have their wits about them. One chap in Cheltenham used to make a living out of waiting until the counter clerk was busy, hand in a twenty pence bet, then adamantly insist he had handed over a £1 coin, and demand the change. When he had exhausted all the town's bookies he moved on to pastures new and tried his trick on supermarkets.

Then there was the ruse known as the 'slow count'. This was to make a bet on a fancied greyhound for £150 or so and only hand in £80 – all in £1 notes. While the counter clerk has been working through the bundle the punter has been listening closely to the commentary, so he has a fair idea how his dog is running. If it is still in with a good chance, he hands over the other £70 in tenners. But if the dog has been obstructed on a bend, or has slipped up, he retires gracefully to the back of the shop – and makes a hurried exit … still with £70 in his pocket.

Then there is the other trick with the dogs, usually tried when there is a horse race timed within a couple of minutes of a dog race – say the 3.30 from Wolverhampton and the 3.32 from Hackney.

If the horse race is slightly late, the commentary from Hackney will be heard first and the result announced … 'Trap one the winner.' Now most dog punters don't write the dog's name on their betting slip, just the trap number. But our con man will write out the dog's name (knowing it has won) in the hope that the counter clerk will throw it in with the betting slips for the Wolverhampton horse race and the settler won't query the timing when the winnings are worked out later.

A journalist had been trying for weeks to pin Lester down to a five-minute exclusive interview on the forthcoming Epsom Derby. He finally collared Lester on the steps of the weighing room in between races at the big York meeting in May.

'Now about this interview, Lester. Just five minutes – that's all I need.'

'Make it two minutes,' said Lester.

'Okay, two minutes then. Now, do you think you'll win the Derby?'

Lester ummed and aahed, gazed around him and stroked his chin. After the full two minutes he turned to the interviewer.

'Yes,' he said – and walked off.

One of the oldest yarns which has done the rounds of the Press rooms is the one about Lester being tapped for a tenner by the lad who'd led up the horse which won the big race with the man himself aboard.

The lad finally caught up with Lester in the racecourse car park.

'What about that tenner, Lester?' said the lad eagerly.

'What?' said Lester.

'The tenner, Lester – you said you'd see me right.'

'I can't hear you, that's my deaf side,' Lester said, reaching his car and hoping to escape the demand.

Quick as a flash, the lad darted round to Lester's other side. 'Lester, you said you'd bung us twenty quid.'

'Cheeky monkey,' came the reply, 'it was only a tenner a second ago.'

Willie Lefebve is the Press Association's northern-based jockeys' reporter whose main duty is sorting out who rides what for the next day's racing. Needless to say, Willie could have retired a wealthy man by now for all the winning rides he has put in the way of jockeys – if only he got an agent's cut of the proceedings!

Lester rang him one day to tell him his horse for a big race at Ayr on the Saturday was a non-runner and did he know if there were any other horses down to run without a jockey. It transpired that there were two, although one was doubtful.

'Lester then told me that the owner of the definite runner had asked him to ride. I saw the trainer of the horse the next day and told him about the owner wanting to put Lester up. The trainer said that was fine by him so I notified the papers that Lester would ride.

'Come the big day and I bumped into the owner in the paddock. It so happened he had never spoken to Lester in his life – although of course he was delighted to have him ride the horse.

'The horse in question didn't win but I think the moral of the story is that if Lester fancied a ride in a particular race, he'd use every trick in the book to get that ride. After all, isn't that partly what made him so successful?'

On another occasion a trainer asked Willie to see if Lester would ride his horse at Chester in the fifth race.

'I approached Lester but he said he wanted to get away after the fourth because he wanted to miss the traffic, which is notorious at Chester. I stuck my neck out, because although I wasn't that convinced myself, I told Lester he ought to look at the horse's form – I was sure it would run well.

'Anyway, Lester relented and said he would ride it. I was on tenterhooks in case it ran badly and I had visions of Lester trying to find me to give me a dressing down. I needn't have worried – Lester worked his old magic on the horse and won by a neck. I'd never been more relieved to see him ride a winner in my life.'

Most trainers would have given their right arm to have Lester up on their horses, and the same can be said of most owners. If a trainer got Lester's services it was a feather in his cap; so you can imagine that Willie saw the possibilities when he was asked by Lester if there was a spare ride going in a race in Newcastle. He darted off to inform the trainer of the only spare horse that Lester would like the ride.

The trainer was not at the races that day and was represented by his wife. Her reaction to Willie's great news shook him to the core. 'Okay,' she said, 'but I'll have to check with the owner.'

From another pressman comes the story of the well-known Northern trainer's unique way of telling his owner to go for a big touch with his horse. It was the night before the race and the owner was anxiously awaiting the phone call which would tell him to put his money down or not. This is how the brief phone call went:

Trainer: 'Good evening, Bill, and how are you?'

Owner: 'I'm very well, very well indeed.'

Trainer: 'Aye, so you might be – but you're not half as well as your horse!'

There was the long-suffering Fleet Street reporter who, having unfailingly bought dinner for Lester on every occasion they had met for the supposedly big exclusive, one night began to nudge the bill inch by inch towards Lester's plate. Finally, Lester picked it up, looked at it, and said: 'That's outrageous. I'd query it if I were you.'

York is Lester's favourite racecourse in the north and it's not difficult to see why. The Knavesmire rivals any of the southern tracks for amenities and when it comes to value for money it leaves them standing. Clerk of the Course and Secretary John Sanderson is one of the men responsible for playing a major part in keeping York racecourse at the top of the tree. Now John is a pretty sharp cookie in the nicest possible sense and has never been backward coming forward to promote his track, providing that it is done with taste and panache. But even he has to admit to a certain amount of marvelling at one of Lester's cute tricks when it came to what might be termed 'the utilization of opportunities'.

'This goes back to the days when we always used to put the picture of the previous year's big-race winner on this year's racecard. So we are talking about 1970 when Lester had won the '69 Magnet Cup on My Swanee and his picture appeared on the front of the card in full colour. At the end of the meeting Lester asked me if I had any spare racecards. It seemed a bit of an odd request but I thought "What the hell?" and let him have a couple of dozen and didn't think any more about it. The following year I was down in London at a dinner arranged by Johnny Walker who were then sponsoring the Ebor which Lester had won the previous season on Tintagel II – putting up three pounds overweight as well. The company had flown in one of their Swiss distributors who had sold more of the whisky than any other of their customers. This chap happened to be a Lester Piggott fan and as we talked he produced two paintings – one of Karabas, the other of Park Top – and a photograph of Lester winning the Ebor on Tintagel II. He asked me if I thought I could get Lester to sign all three.

'So we came round to the Tuesday of the Ebor meeting and I saw Lester and asked if he would sign these pictures and the photograph. As he signed them I could almost hear his mind ticking over. "Is this the picture of me and Tintagel that's going to be on this Thursday's racecard?" he asked me. I told him it was. "How many cards can you spare?" he then asked. Of course, I then remembered that he had asked for the racecards which had featured him and My Swanee. "Well they come to us from Weatherby's in packs of five hundred," I told him. "Five hundred would do nicely," replied Lester.

'Ebor day came and I put aside a pack of five hundred. Lester came and picked them up and was just walking away with them when my curiosity got the better of me: "Lester, may I ask what you're going to do with them all?"

'"Same as with the others," said Lester. "I cut out the pictures, autograph them and send them off to all the people who write to me requesting a photograph!"'

There was the true story about a famous jockey-turned-trainer who had just saddled the winner of his first big race. All smiles after the presentation in the winner's enclosure, the trainer and his wife were asked if they would care to go up to the stewards' room to celebrate their success. The odds were enormous. 'You must be laughing,' said the senior steward. 'How much did you have on?'

'Not a penny!' the trainer's wife chipped in. 'He hasn't had a bet since he stopped riding.'

Channel Four television presenter Jim McGrath, who has even more hats than Royal Ascot's Mrs Shilling, was wearing his Timeform cap when he shared a plane with Piggott and several other jockeys on their way to Longchamp for the big Prix Vermeille meeting, held in September.

Lester had five rides that day so was naturally anxious to be there in good time. The disappointment came, however, when the pilot announced that there was fog at Le Bourget Airport, north east of Paris, and an instrument landing was out of the question.

Being the good journalist he is, Jim was at pains to observe the various jockeys' reactions. One of our younger top-class riders said he didn't want to fly anywhere if there was a hint of danger. Another wondered if they could wait a while until the fog cleared.

Not Lester though. Having organized the plane in the first place and not wanting to miss any of his rides, he came up with the solution: 'We'll just have to land in a field.'

Off they flew with Lester firmly ensconced in the co-pilot's seat. Over the Channel and on to Paris, only to find that the fog had still not cleared.

'There's nothing we can do but circle,' said the pilot, much to Lester's annoyance.

For a moment Jim thought Lester was going to take over the controls himself – 'I'm sure he would have done if he could.' So they circled ... and circled. Eventually the weather cleared and they made a perfect landing much to everyone else's relief. Lester, on the other hand, was furious. The plane had not stopped its taxi run to the apron before he flung open the door, leapt out and sprinted for the terminal building and a waiting taxi – pausing only to shout over his shoulders, 'Too bloody late!'

Persistent pressmen have long been a thorn in Lester's side but over the years he has learned to live with the many questions with which he is often bombarded. As a younger man, however, woe betide anyone who caught him in the wrong mood.

Lester had attracted a lot of media attention since his 'Boy Wonder' days and his brushes with the authorities. In 1962, at the age of twenty-six, he was riding in a seller for selling race specialist Bob Ward at a Lincoln evening fixture. It was just a week before the Epsom Derby.

Ward had two runners in the race and when the betting opened Lester's mount Ione was made favourite. But stable companion Polly Macaw's odds soon began to tumble and she was installed favourite at the off. In the race Lester knew his filly had no chance of winning. She was, as he described, 'useless' and this was what she subsequently proved.

The stewards, however, accused Lester and his trainer of 'pulling' Ione – even though Lester was adamant that she would never have beaten Polly Macaw in a month of Sundays – and the matter was referred to Portman Square.

The outcome of the meeting of the Jockey Club made headlines – Ward's licence was withdrawn and Lester was suspended until the end of July. He was livid by the time he arrived home to Newmarket after attending the disciplinary hearing.

There at the front door was the posse of journalists – doing what their newsdesks demanded but still the last thing Lester wanted to see. As they besieged his house, Lester's patience finally wore thin. One reporter was socked squarely on the chin. Then he scattered the rest of the 'pack' by throwing stones at them from his garden.

There was a well-known steward's secretary, admired by all and sundry for his forthright views, keen eye and extensive knowledge of all the tricks of the trade.

A top rider of the time thought he had just made a good job of giving a particular horse a 'quiet' run during a race. That was until the steward's secretary took him by the arm on his way back to the weighing room and told him in no uncertain manner: 'For Christ's sake, if you want to pull a horse – keep your f— elbows going.'

The fifteen-year-old Lester was invited to ride out with the string of a Lambourn trainer noted as a disciplinarian. When the horses reached the Downs, however, Lester and the three-year-old colt were missing and it was several minutes before the schoolboy trotted up quietly, and rejoined the rest. 'And where do you think you've been?' exclaimed the trainer in full flow. 'Sorry sir,' said Lester shyly, 'he was playing up and I thought it would do him good to jump a few hurdles.'

'What! He's never jumped a hurdle in his life,' said the trainer.

'He has now,' smiled Lester.

A journalist had been out with Lester in his car during an afternoon's interview for an in-depth piece for a forthcoming colour supplement. As they were pulling into Lester's drive in the Mercedes, they saw a loose horse standing by the gate. 'Don't you think we should catch it?' the journalist inquired.

'No,' said Lester emphatically. 'Never catch a loose horse – you could end up holding the bloody thing all day.'

Lester was flying across the English Channel on his way back from France and was sitting in the co-pilot's seat. Suddenly the pilot tapped him on the shoulder and pointed to an oil tanker below that was on fire. 'Let's take a look,' said Lester. The plane swooped down until it was almost over the scene. Lester turned to the pilot and, gesturing the plane upwards once more, quipped: 'It's all right – it's not one of mine.'

Lester, a great supporter of many charities, was once asked by Bolsover Comprehensive School in Derbyshire if he could spare a personal item for a fund-raising auction.

Lester promptly despatched an old sock – and it helped raise money for a school mini-bus!

Mike Watt, Lester's manager, once upset him when they were doing a deal with a pottery firm over some limited edition souvenir artefacts regarding Lester's retirement. The firm sent down a team for a photographic session at Lester's home and they all gathered outside near the stables. The director of the unit said they would like some casual shots, showing the type of things Lester wears around the yard when he's in 'civvies' as opposed to his riding silks. The message was relayed to Lester and he eventually came out of his house wearing slacks and a sweater. Mike thought the sweater looked a bit 'naff' — so he said so: 'Aren't you going to put on a decent sweater?' he asked.

Lester looked most upset, gave a quick glance down at the sweater and said: 'It's my best. It's real cashmere and it cost me four hundred quid.'

There was a lengthy stewards' inquiry after a race at Goodwood in which Lester was involved. The Press gathered outside the stewards' room anxiously awaiting the outcome. At last Lester emerged grim-faced.

'What happened, Lester?' the cry went up in unison. 'Give us a hundred pounds and I'll tell you,' said Lester.

The result of the inquiry was that Lester had just been fined £100.

A well-known journalist had ordered a taxi to take him to the airport after racing at Longchamp when Lester asked for a lift and jumped in the back. The journalist was delighted at being in such close proximity to the mighty man whom he normally only saw in much different circumstances.

As the taxi was pulling up outside the terminal, the journalist put his hand in his pocket for his money to pay the fare. Almost at the same time, Lester did exactly the same.

'No, no, Lester,' said the journalist, 'have this on the paper.'

It was only then that Lester gave him a querulous look, pulled out a large apple, bit into it — and got out without saying a word.

It was one of those dreadful wet spring days at York when the skies were grey as slate. It was absolutely throwing it down. But there was some good racing in store and a steady stream of slow-moving traffic stretched almost as far back as the A1. Lester, driving his Mercedes, was in no mood to miss the first race because of it.

Near the course itself it was even worse. After a couple of smart manoeuvres, Lester managed to reach the car park entrance. There,

however, stood a large Yorkshire bobby with his hand outstretched beckoning Lester's car to stop. He had just witnessed the Mercedes' erratic charge.

Lester stopped the car just as the officer reached into his sodden top pocket and produced an equally wet notebook. At the same time he gestured for Lester to open his window. Lester pressed the electric button and the window opened a few inches.

'Ah, I know you,' the bobby shouted in his unmistakable Yorkshire accent, 'you're a bloody maniac, shouldn't be on the roads, a bloody fool that's what you are.'

Lester pressed the window button again and opened it a little further to get a good sight of the officer, who was looking totally fed up, with the rain dripping off the end of his nose and running down the back of his tunic.

'Well,' said Lester, 'it all depends on what you mean by a bloody fool. There you are soaked to the skin and getting wetter by the minute and here am I nice and dry in my lovely warm car – which do you think is the bloody fool?'

It stopped the officer in his tracks. 'Get on,' he shouted stuffing his notebook back in his pocket and waving the car through, 'get on.'

As Lester has admitted, he sometimes got things wrong. But we all know he got it right more often than not. Like the day his wife Susan was entertaining a client of her bloodstock agency at their Newmarket home. Lester walked into the house and was introduced.

'What's going to win the big race at the weekend, Lester?' said the client.

The big race was Europe's richest, the Prix de l'Arc de Triomphe at Longchamp, and Lester was riding the Robert Sangster colt Alleged. Vincent O'Brien had specifically aimed him at an autumn campaign, considering him a little too backward compared to The Minstrel.

'I'll win it on Alleged,' said Lester confidently.

'What will be second and third?' the client teased.

Without blinking, Lester replied: 'Balmerino, the New Zealand-bred horse, will be second and the Queen's filly, Dunfermline, will possibly be third.'

And the result? Alleged the winner, Balmerino second and Dunfermline beaten a short head for third place.

Famous last words by Sir Gordon Richards half-way through the 1960 season: 'If only Lester was seven pounds lighter he would certainly top the jockeys' list. As it is, I very much doubt if he will make it.'

At the end of the season Lester won the first of his eleven Jockeys' Championships.

Famous last words by a racing correspondent in 1954: 'Lester, who is now eighteen, is still growing and it may well be that he has ridden his last race on the Flat. Next season I expect him to turn to jumping in which weight is less important. And in any case he had not expected to continue Flat racing for more than another two years.'

CHAPTER FIVE
FOREIGN FIELDS

I was lucky enough to have travelled the world during my career. I met all sorts of people, rode at some strange tracks – and had a lot of fun.

In the 1983 season I rode two winners at the tiny Les Landes track in Jersey during their big race-night for the Rothmans Trophy. Being such a small place, its facilities are pretty basic and while I was getting changed in the jockeys' room I asked some of the local riders about the track.

One of them told me that the course was 'like the wall of death' and said that if my horse cocked its jaw and went straight on at the first bend we'd be right over the cliff top. Another rider told me to be careful at the start – they don't have starting stalls, just a piece of elastic that twangs across the field to set them on their way. This jockey told me that if I was on the outside when we lined up then I'd better be careful, ''cos the elastic's likely to rattle you one round the ear 'ole if you try to jump off too quickly'.

The following season Willie Carson was invited over and he too rode a double. I think the local lads tried to put him off as well, though knowing Willie I'm sure he had an answer for them. In 1985 Yves St Martin went there and rode one winner and, as Willie and I had found, he was up against some good women riders in some of the races. Next time we saw Yves we pulled his leg about it – someone told him it didn't take much to beat him in a finish. I can't remember whether he was beaten by a woman or not – mind you, they are very competent ladies over there – but we had a good laugh about it all the same.

They take their racing very seriously in Jersey and there is a great rivalry between the local owners and trainers and those who come over from Guernsey. After the evening's racing I met some of the Jersey Race Club officials and also the Rothmans organizer. When I was leaving the course, there was a beautiful red sky out to sea. The Rothmans man looked at the

sunset, shook his head admiringly, and said: 'That's a wonderful sight –
the Jersey people say it means Guernsey's on fire!'

When I was in another country I had to watch my diet perhaps more
carefully than I did at home. I always found that I could eat one meal a day
but I would never eat too much, just small quantities. Ice-cream was one of
my favourite dishes to help keep the hunger pangs away. When I was in
Australia a couple of years ago I discovered these ice-cream-jelloe sticks
called Paddle-Pops – they're the best thing Aussie had produced since
Phar-Lap!

The ice-cream is good in America too – they have a thousand and one
different flavours. One of the best presents I got was in a hotel in San
Francisco where a squad of British jockeys were riding against a team of
American jockeys. I went into the hotel restaurant for a glass of water and
came out with a bag of about two hundred lollipops – they give them free to
the kids who go in with their parents. Well, the girl at the counter did tell
me to help myself . . . talk about Kojak!

One of the trips I used to look forward to was our annual visit to the States,
usually around the end of November. I was captain of a team of All-Star
jockeys on several occasions when we rode at The Meadowlands in New
Jersey against a team of American jockeys.

The tracks out there are pretty much the same configuration – all are left-
handed and oval with most of the racing on dirt. The facilities are a
different world to all but one or two of the very best tracks in Britain. At
The Meadowlands, which is just across the Hudson from Manhattan, there
are three different restaurants, all with ideal viewing. In fact you don't even
need to leave your seat to watch the races or have a bet – there's a television
set placed at every conceivable angle and a host of pretty girls taking the
punters' money with a smile.

One year Greville Starkey was with us and he was riding on dirt for the
first time . . . it was like that old advert where the guy got sand kicked in his
face.

After a bit of work on the course on the first morning Greville was a bit
subdued afterwards. He'd been directly behind another horse sending the
dirt at him full pelt. He looked in the mirror at the red blotches on his face.
'That stuff really stings,' he said. 'It's like hailstones.'

I think it was a bit of a shock to him. Like the horses themselves, he soon got used to the idea; though somehow I think he hankered for Goodwood and the luscious green turf of the Sussex Downs.

After myself, Greville was the next senior jockey riding on a regular daily basis. I suppose his sense of humour was a bit like mine in a way. He often had a straight face but, as I often said about myself, inside he was laughing.

Greville's favourite trick is to bark like a dog. He's been doing this party piece for so long now that on occasions I even had to turn round to see if it was the real thing. It comes across as a bad-tempered little terrier and Greville's had some hilarious moments producing his dog.

Once when Greville was riding in Argentina a few years ago for the All-Stars, Greville soon had the racegoers eating out of his hand. He was at the San Isidro track in Buenos Aires and the match against South American jockeys was over a period of two days. As Greville was cantering his first ride to the post he passed close to the stands at the far end of the grandstand

where there was a large group of racegoers leaning on the rails watching the runners go past.

Greville went past and started his barking routine – they all looked stunned at first. But on each of his subsequent rides they all waited for him to go past then started barking back and laughing and cheering. Greville got a big kick out of that – the funny side of a serious match against the Argentinians.

Henry Cecil used to tell the story of the night they went to dinner with Greville after he had won a big race at Deauville in the summer of 1973 aboard the filly Katie Cecil, who was named after Julie and Henry's daughter, Katrina.

After flying back to London, the victorious party decided to go to a rather upmarket London restaurant. Greville had been riding light that day and the couple of glasses of fine wine must have gone to his head, because he suddenly started the barking routine. The guests in the restaurant included some VIPs who seemed far from amused. But the 'terrier' just wouldn't stop his barking and growling throughout the remainder of the meal.

After they had settled their bill, Henry must have thought he couldn't be any more embarrassed so he took hold of one of the napkins, rolled it into a loop, and led Greville out of the place on all fours still barking like mad on the 'lead'.

An interesting thing about Henry is that he never uses binoculars these days and has developed a keen eyesight for watching the field for the last half mile or so. Like Henry, there are a few trainers around who only like to hear about any trouble in running after the race is over and who claim that the finish is the most important part.

I think it all stems from the days when Henry lost half a dozen pairs of very expensive binoculars in a period of just a few months – usually left behind in bars during, as he says 'my days of gin and lime'.

Perhaps he got fed up with the forms for the insurers – they certainly did!

I've had brushes with officials all over the world and it's usually been a case of making an issue out of what I believed was a raw deal. In the mid-seventies I was riding at a place called Scottsville near Durban in South Africa. I was aboard a heavily-backed favourite, a horse called The

Maltster. The starter pressed the button but the stalls didn't all open at once and so I gave him a piece of my mind because I'd been left ten lengths adrift.

Luckily, The Maltster was a very good horse and I managed to get him up with the others and we eventually went on to win the race — I think by a length. But if he'd not been such a decent animal we would have trailed in through no fault of our own and then the punters would have been howling for my blood — in fact I believed they would have been entitled to have asked for their money back.

When I got back to the weighing room I found that the starter had reported me to the stewards for swearing at him and in the end they fined me £280. I thought it was ridiculous — if it had happened at a European track and the horse had lost they would have burned the place down!

They get very upset on the Continent when there is such an important thing as money at stake. There was a riot at Longchamp one year and the police had to be called in after a big race I had ridden in, the Prix d'Ispahan. I was on that very good racemare Trillion who had won at Longchamp no less than seven times and had finished runner-up to Alleged when I rode Robert Sangster's horse to win his second Arc in 1978.

Trillion was bred and owned by Nelson Bunker-Hunt, for whom I had ridden such good horses as Youth, Exceller and Dahlia, and I had a soft spot for her because her sire was also the sire of Roberto on whom I had that last-gasp win in the Derby of 1972.

In the Longchamp race Irish River was the 5–4 favourite but a lot of people obviously fancied Trillion to run well and coupled her with the favourite in forecasts on Le Tiercé — the French tote. I came third to Irish River and Philippe Paquet's mount, a horse called Opus Dei, but the riders of the fourth and fifth objected to Philippe's horse and this gave the punters some hope of a pay-off: with Opus Dei relegated I would have been placed second and their winning bets would have come up trumps.

At the subsequent inquiry the stewards not only threw out Opus Dei — but Trillion as well. And to rub salt into my wounds, they gave me and Philippe a four-day ban.

The punters went wild. There was a gang of about two hundred of them around the parade ring causing so much noise that the runners for the next race had to be taken back to the stables. Another group went on to the track and the police had to remove them. Then they started throwing stones and debris at the officials – in fact anything they could lay their hands on. It was pandemonium for about half an hour ... Talk about the storming of the Bastille!

Another time at the same track there was a big rumpus when course officials began protesting after one of their colleagues had been given the sack. I remember the day well – it was a particularly painful one for me.

I had just got the leg up on a horse called Tender Night when the protesters began their racket, shouting, banging tin cans, a right commotion. Tender Night spooked and reared, throwing me to the ground with a terrific thump. I remounted again and went on to the track but rather than turn around and go past the stands where the protesters had begun their chanting again, I thought I'd go the long way round to the start so my horse wouldn't spook again.

I'd just set off when this clown of an official ran out on to the track. He thought I had made a mistake and started waving his arms at me – a Frenchman doing his impersonation of a windmill. My horse took one look at him, spooked and reared up again, dumping me on the turf and, for good measure, kicking me in the back. I had to receive medical treatment and Tender Night was withdrawn. Fortunately I was able to ride in later races but if it hadn't hurt when I laughed, I might have had a good chuckle at the irony of it.

All the good times make up for the bad ones and a few years earlier, the October of 1973 to be exact, I was rewarded with one of my most memorable moments when Rheingold won the Prix de l'Arc de Triomphe. After I had beaten Rheingold on Roberto in the Derby I was never too confident of a rematch because I admired Rheingold's toughness. So I was delighted to ride him in the following year's Arc against those great fillies Dahlia and Allez France, even though Dahlia had already beaten Rheingold in the King George VI and Queen Elizabeth Diamond Stakes at Ascot that year.

I had never won the Arc before, but not for want of trying – I was second on Sir Ivor, Park Top and Nijinsky. As soon as I sat on Rheingold in the paddock I knew he was ready to run the best race of his life. I had ridden him in two bits of work in the run-up to the big day and I could tell he was improving fast. Now, on the way to the start, I was almost laughing to myself – he really felt that good and I was convinced we would win. It was a big field, with twenty-six other runners, so I kept him handy, then went for it before the two-furlong marker. At the line we had two and a half lengths

to spare over the second horse Allez France and a further four lengths over
Hard To Beat, who was third. It was a marvellous day and Rheingold's
trainer Barry Hills had done an absolute peach of a job in producing the
horse at his very best.

   Something that tickled me to learn about Rheingold was that his dam
Athene was so useless as a racehorse that at the end of her two-year-old
days she was given as a prize in a Saints and Sinners raffle – and the
tickets were just a quid!

The thing about riding all over the world was that the amount of travelling often meant I was working to a very tight schedule, so much so that the riding was always the easy part. Most years I reckoned I did about 300,000 miles, so there was obviously a great amount of organizing involved. Once I was riding in a place called Albany in Western Australia, about three hundred miles or so from Perth, but I had to be in Singapore the next day where I was riding in a big race.

The problem was that I was riding in Albany's 2.30 p.m. race and the only flight from Perth to Singapore was at 3.45 p.m. – and even by jet Albany was a good hour from Perth. I rode in the race, jumped off the horse almost as we pulled up and legged it to a waiting chartered jet still in my silks. Within sixty seconds we were airborne and I was able to fling my riding clothes off and get changed into my 'civvies'. The jet touched down at Perth and I then had to run across the apron to the big Qantas airliner. They slammed the door shut behind me and we were off for Singapore. After winning the Singapore event I flew on to Hong Kong where I was riding the next day in a jockeys' invitation race.

The good thing about it all was that I won on all three rides – not a bad long-distance hat-trick if you ask me.

Lester was staying at the Hilton Hotel in Kuala Lumpur one year during a spell of riding in Malaysia. After racing one day he was returning to the hotel, which is opposite the track, with former Hong Kong trainer, Frank Carr.

They arrived just in time to see the fire engines rolling up and smoke billowing out of the windows.

'Good God,' said Frank, 'the place is on fire.'

Lester was watching, laconically. Finally he muttered: 'I hope they can save my cigars.'

Another time in the Far East, Lester and Susan flew into Singapore from Hong Kong. Their plane was late arriving which meant Lester had only a few minutes to get to the Bukit Timah racecourse where he was riding in the big race, the Lion City Cup.

Anyone who has experience of airports and immigration knows about officialdom. If Lester had waited like everyone else, he would have missed his ride. So, not to be outdone by the line of people waiting to go through immigration and passport control, Lester took matters into his own hands, vaulted the barrier, ran hell-for-leather out of the terminal building and jumped into the nearest cab. He was away before the astonished officials could do anything about it.

The officials descended on Susan, who tried to explain the position. But they refused to release Lester's passport, demanding that he return personally to pick it up.

Lester duly won the race on a horse named Blue Star and he and Susan had dinner that night with a friend, Jacob Ballas, who'd lived all his life in Singapore and knew anyone who was anyone on the island.

Half-way through the meal, Lester, who obviously didn't relish the hassle of returning to passport control (with perhaps a ticking off for good measure), hit on the perfect solution.

'Jacob,' he said winningly, 'you know everyone on the island who is important: you're the man to go and get my passport.'

Jacob wasn't so sure.

Folkestone was high on Lester's list as one of the most unlikeable tracks in Britain. When he went to Hong Kong for the opening of the multi-million-dollar Shah Tin racecourse, which had been built by slicing the top off a mountain and using the earth to reclaim the land from the sea, Lester was collared by a Hong Kong TV reporter who asked him if Shah Tin reminded him of any British racecourse.

'Yeah,' said Lester, 'Folkestone.'

The late Brian Taylor was riding in Italy for the first time and accompanied Lester on the plane to Milan. 'What are these Italian jockeys like, Lester?' Brian asked. 'Stupid,' replied Lester, 'just take no notice of them.'

During one race in which they were both riding, an Italian jockey tried to put Lester over the rails but, sharp as ever, Lester gave his horse a yank on the reins and it was the Italian who collided with the running rail. At that stage Brian loomed upsides. 'See what I mean?' called Lester.

With difficult horses in mind, there is a fascinating tale told by Charlie Rose. Charlie has worked with horses all his life and is now assistant trainer to John Veitch in New York. It was when John was training for Calumet Farm that Charlie teamed up with a horse called Rivalero. The horse came to Calumet Farm's barn at Belmont Park as a two-year-old in 1978, that historic year when the stable's Alydar had finished runner-up to Affirmed in the US Triple Crown races. Charlie rode Alydar in all his work and accompanied him wherever he raced. Rivalero, on the other hand, was gelded despite the fact that he cost $170,000 as a yearling at the Saratoga Sales. In his first start Rivalero tried to savage the winner and finished runner-up, a pattern that repeated itself next time out when just beaten by Secretariat's son, General Assembly.

Charlie quickly formed the opinion that Rivalero, who was by Riva Ridge out of a Bold Ruler mare, did not like racing and would sooner fool around. It might sound silly, but Rivalero was a showman, an extrovert whose antics would bring staff from other barns running out to watch and take pictures – and he loved it and played to his audience. His favourite trick was to catch hold of the reins in his mouth so that Charlie would be powerless to do anything, then he would stand up straight on his hind legs or try some other means of throwing his rider off. Then, at the last moment, he would duck his shoulder and catch Charlie safe and sound. There were only two moments in all their time together that Rivalero actually dumped Charlie on the floor – once when a chicken flew off a rail in front of him and another time when a horse and rider came galloping towards them on the exercise track at Saratoga.

After the latter episode, Rivalero was just about to gallop off riderless when his trainer, who was standing at the side of the track, called out his name: 'Hey Reeve, come here fella.' The gelding did just that, walking over as meekly as a kitten.

One summer at Belmont on their way to the track for the morning workout, Charlie took Rivalero a different route, one that passed by the main road on the other side of the perimeter wire fence. Rivalero stood and watched the trucks and cars on the highway for a good ten minutes, standing stock still. Charlie took him that same route all the time after that, each day standing and watching the traffic flow.

One of the horse's favourite tricks was at Hialeah in Florida where many of the Veitch horses go for the winter. Outside each barn was a large 'trash' can and on his way to the track or on his way back, he would try to get as close as he could to one then lash out and send it and the contents flying all over the place. He also loved to kick water buckets off their stools.

On the racecourse he would soon assess the opposition. If they were not up to much he'd put his head down and gallop, winning by ten lengths or more. If he was in better class company he would sulk and dig his toes in. He wasn't the best horse Veitch and Charlie have trained but he was certainly the funniest character of a horse they have ever come across. When Rivalero wanted, he could be a good horse – he won something like fifteen races and almost half a million dollars prize money . . . not bad for a 'rogue'.

One of Rose's most poignant memories in the whole of his career was the day he went to Kentucky to see Alydar. They say that some horses remember the special people in their lives and this visit proved the point. On arriving, Alydar was at the far end of the paddock. One of the stud hands saw Charlie leaning on the rail: 'You'll never get to see him standing there,' he said, 'he only ever stands the other side of the paddock.'

Charlie took no notice however, and called out: 'Hey Al.' Alydar pricked his ears and came galloping over at full speed causing Charlie to worry that his old friend was going to collide with the rails. In all his years with horses, Charlie had to admit that he had never seen anything like this as Alydar nuzzled up to him, then began bucking and kicking and squealing. He caused so much of a racket that staff from the stud rushed out thinking there was something wrong with the horse but it was just that he was so happy to be seeing his pal once more. After a few minutes however, Charlie had to leave: 'I sure had a lump in my throat and a tear in my eye. I just had to leave – I didn't want a forty-million-dollar stallion injuring himself because of old Charlie Rose.'

When Roy David was looking after the worldwide publicity for the Rothmans International in Toronto from 1981 to 1984, he teamed up with one of racing's greatest living characters, the Irishman Jack Doyle, who handled the race entries. What Jack doesn't know about buying horses could be written on the back of a losing Tote ticket although the man himself will be the first to say that he knows very little about the game even though he's been in it most of his life as amateur rider, trainer and bloodstock agent. Before switching to buying mainly Flat horses, Jack's golden touch was associated with jumpers and he bought the likes of Deep Run, Pollardstown and the best of the lot, Mill House.

Jack was convinced he had a future champion on his hands when he picked up Mill House from his friends the Lawlors, who bred the horse at Naas. Trying to sell the gelding for £6,500, however, was another matter and even the likes of Ryan Price, Frenchie Nicholson and Fred Rimell thought him too expensive. Eventually Jack found an owner in Bill Gollings and the horse went to be trained by the ex-Ryan Price head lad Sid Dale. Then Jack sat back and waited for the day he would have a giant punt. His chance soon came, for the horse was running at Wincanton and Jack's team of punter friends turned up to join in the gamble. In the parade ring Sid told Mill House's jockey Ron Harrison not to be hard on the horse and to give him a nice school finishing fifth or sixth. When Jack heard this he dashed off to see his punter friends and told them the horse wasn't off. Sure enough, the boys kept their money in their pockets and Mill House drifted to 3–1.

When the horses were at the start, Sid turned to Jack in the stands and said: 'If this horse was doing his best today how much would you be having on?' Jack replied he'd be parting with a thousand pounds. 'Well you'd better get on quick then,' said Sid.

Jack was horror-struck at the thought of his boys missing out and made to dash down and tell them. But Sid grabbed him by the throat and said: 'No you don't, you b—.' He had sussed out Jack's boys and didn't want them battering down the horse's price.

In the end Jack just had time to get his own money on, Mill House skated home – and Jack was very nearly lynched by his group of punters who went home to Ireland with their tails between their legs.

Jockey Alan Bond recalls the day he rode in the Spanish Derby in Madrid – and discovered the lengths to which some foreign riders would go to put one over on the greatest jockey in the world.

'They didn't have an inside running rail at this track – just a privet hedge – and if you get a belt during the race you can end up going straight through it. We jumped off and Lester kicked his horse into the inside position and was hugging the hedge in about fourth or fifth position. This Spanish rider on Lester's outside then began to knock Lester's horse into the hedge every few strides. Soon there were leaves and bits of privet flying everywhere as Lester kept getting bump after bump all the way round and I could see he was in trouble. We were just passing the stands for the first time and there was a tremendous crowd there – all the grandstands were completely full. Well, Lester must have got fed up with this treatment and who could blame him? He suddenly lifted up his whip and gave the guy three whacks across his back.

'I was about six horses back and even I could feel it. The jockey obviously got the message because he moved out of the way but he stood up in his irons and started screaming. Then there was uproar, the crowd was shouting, this jockey was cursing in Spanish, and Lester had to be almost ushered back to the weighing room. Once inside, Lester was most unconcerned but this jockey was trying to have a go at him while all sorts of people were holding him back. All Lester said was: "Where are my colours for the next race?" and continued changing as if nothing had happened.

'Just before he went out for the next race, Lester gave me a wink and said: "I had to do that – he wouldn't understand anything else." A week later I was riding in Madrid again and I discovered Lester had been fined £100 for the incident. I saw him the following week during racing and told him the outcome. He just shrugged and said: "That's okay – the owner will pay."'

Lester and Susan and Mike and Gay Watt went to Madrid where Lester
was riding for a Spanish-based owner, Bobby Ionescu. We'll let Mike take
up the story:

'Lester had been riding in Paris on the Saturday and we were flying to
Madrid from there. When we got to the airport our plane was delayed,
then there was a big queue waiting to check in, all that sort of thing. Of
course, Lester just walked straight to the top of the queue – that was when
I realized he doesn't like to be kept hanging about.

'We eventually landed in Madrid and it was pouring down, and I mean
raining. The owner was there to meet us and all the introductions were
made as we made our way out of the terminal building towards where I
thought the cars would be parked. I could see Señor Ionescu counting the
party and when we got outside he called a taxi, gave instructions to the
driver and ushered Lester, Susan and Gay into it. Then he turned to me
and said that I looked like a sporting fellow. Well, the taxi had gone and I
thought to myself, aye, aye, perhaps we're going to do a quick tour of the
red light district of Madrid before we catch up with the others – it was the
way he said it.

'As we were walking over to the car park he was telling me that this
was the first rain they had seen for months. I think the weather must
have been saving it specially for this day because when we got to the car
park all I could see was this open-sided mini-moke. He put on his mac and
a hat which he tilted at the jauntiest of angles over his ear, then invited
me to jump in. The seats were already wet and I hung on like grim death
as he screeched away out of the airport. The first truck that went past us
in the opposite direction absolutely drenched me – it sent up a wave of
rain water from a ditch in the road.

'Señor Ionescu was having a ball, driving this thing for all it was worth.
Another truck went past us, then another, until I was like a drowned rat.
He looked at me and shouted above the roar of the engine: "If Sir Lester
had got pneumonia he would not have been able to ride my horse, yes?"
Jesus, I thought, I'm with a madman here – now it's Sir Lester to boot.

'We roared up to the hotel where we were staying and he jumped out. I
sort of fell out – my trousers were stuck to the seat, my suit was ruined, I
was saturated. I felt a right fool walking into the hotel reception. There
was Lester all dry and comfortable and laughing his head off. He took one
look at me and said: "I heard the guy was a bad driver but I didn't think
you'd wet yourself!"

'We were then all taken for lunch to a large house. Thankfully by this time the rain had stopped and we were gathered in the gardens, long trestle tables around a swimming pool with all the family present. Now Spanish lunches can take all day and the courses keep coming. Obviously we had an eye on the time but there were still six courses to be served. As got to be the habit, I sat next to Lester – and I soon learned why. Lester didn't like to upset his hosts by refusing all this lovely food so he turned to me and said: "Help me out." Then he started passing me most of his food under the table. We started with gazpacho – it was the old bowl swop under the table and I spilled half of it over my shoes. Then came tortilla, the Spanish dish of potato omelette. As it was being served over his shoulder, Lester was in the middle of a conversation and was gesticulating like mad. He knocked the tortilla out of the maid's hand, it did a couple of somersaults in the air, and landed smack on his plate. The whole table shouted "olé" and asked for an encore. Lester kept asking for some of this and some of that while the host sat – as head of the family – at the top of the table, beaming. I was like a stuffed pig and could hardly move by the time we came to go racing – it was a day we've often had a good laugh about. I mean you don't forget times like that in a hurry, not your first trip abroad with Lester!'

There have been many other memorable occasions all over the world since then. Like the time Lester was riding at Santa Anita – with a BBC film crew in tow trying to record the crowd's reaction to Lester winning in America.

'We were on a very tight schedule, something that has always been a part of Lester's life and, boy, can it get chaotic. I had a car waiting at the track and I was driving the pair of us to the airport to catch a plane to Miami where Lester was riding the next day. After his last ride at Santa Anita, Lester came running to the car still in his riding gear and carrying his bag, jumped in the car, and we set off weaving in and out of the traffic, ignoring other drivers' threats and horn-blowing and desperate that we should get to the airport in time.

'So there was Lester in the back trying to get changed and being thrown all round the place. The sight of him with one leg in his underpants as I turned a sharp corner! It's a wonder we weren't done for something under the state laws of decency. He was still struggling to get the other leg in when he said to me: "You're the worst bloody driver I've ever been with." I turned round and told him at that rate he'd be the only deaf pommie millionaire hitching in California. We finally made it anyway and Lester

was just about dressed by the time we got there. It wasn't the first time he used the back of a car as a changing room – planes, boats, trains … you name it.

'About two weeks later we had a spot of business together in London and we were in Lester's car with him driving. As he was swinging in and out of the traffic with his foot down and I was being thrown all over the place I remembered what he had said about my driving in California and I told him he was the worst driver I had ever been with.

'He didn't take his eyes off the road, but just stuck his foot down and swerved round a couple of cars, then smiled and said: "Yeah, and at that rate you'll be the only unemployed Kiwi hitching in Berkeley Square!"'

Mike Watt had not long taken over the commercial management aspect of Lester's career when the two of them met at Paris Airport. After a few quick words Lester had to dash off to catch his plane; before doing so, he thrust an envelope into Mike's hand with the words: 'This is for you.'

It seemed a gift, and not wishing to embarrass Lester by opening the envelope in front of him, Mike waited until he was some way off. It was when he opened the envelope that his face dropped – Lester had presented him with three parking tickets picked up from his weekend in the capital.

Lester was on an overnight flight from Rome to Johannesburg, flying by South African Airlines, and on his way to join a team of All-Star jockeys who were due to ride against a squad of home-based riders. After a previous hectic few days and with the prospect of a busy time ahead, Lester was intent on getting as much rest as possible and had just drifted off into a nice deep sleep when the cabin staff began bringing round breakfast.

Before Mike could signal to the steward that Lester was not to be disturbed, he had shaken Lester to a bleary-eyed consciousness.

'What would you like for breakfast sir?' said the steward, pointing to the array of goodies on a silver platter.

'I don't want anything,' Lester grumbled, immediately closing his eyes to return to the land of nod.

Again the steward shook him. 'But I've been up all night cooking this delicious food,' the steward insisted.

'I don't eat much, I'm a jockey,' Lester mumbled.

The steward thought Lester had said something about 'playing hookey', rather than being a jockey.

'Look,' said the steward, 'hookey, truant, I don't care what you been doin' – you gotta eat my eggs, man.'

With all the travelling around came the receptions, the introductions, the smiles, handshakes and all those sort of things that an introvert like Lester found irksome at times. Sure, he'd sit there and be polite, but often he would sooner have been up in his hotel room having a kip or a dish or ice-cream. Mike recalls how an introductory speaker got carried away during a dinner when Lester was riding in some invitation races in Australia one winter.

'It was a ritzy place packed with VIPs and racing dignitaries. The person who was introducing Lester got up and started talking, and went on and on. Lester was sitting beside me and he was going to have to stand up and say a few words, how happy he was to be there, that sort of thing. Well, half an hour later this guy was still talking and Lester got up and left the room. I thought to myself that he was just dashing off to the men's cloakroom and would be back in a minute. After a couple of minutes I began to get a bit worried and after five minutes I was frantic. Then, what I feared would happen did happen. The guy wound up this long rambling speech and said: "So ladies and gentlemen, I give you Lester Piggott."

'But, of course, there was no Lester Piggott. He had walked out of the place, got into my car, and driven back to the hotel where he went to bed.

Lester had not been able to hear what the speaker was saying because he had gone on for so long, and thought he wasn't needed any longer – I had to stand up and say a few words instead!

'There was a similarly funny incident in San Francisco before the annual All-Stars match at the Bay Meadows track. These occasions are all very glamorous, no-expense spared affairs with all the Press in attendance as well as the jockeys, all with little flags in front of their places representing their country.

'The master of ceremonies this time got into a bit of a pickle when it came to introducing Lester. He started off by saying: "Let's give a big welcome to Sir Lester Piggott and his lovely bride Mau-reen." Maureen is his daughter. Granted, the guy did then change it to Susan so he got that bit right but he then started reading a list of some of the great horses and races with which Lester had been associated. It went something like this, and with a heavy American drawl: "... then there was the Triple Crown with Nigh-Jinsky, Roberto, The Minstrel, Teen-o-so, Florizel, Hamilton Road, Newmarket, England, Kind Regards, Nick Clarke, IRB."

'While Jimmy Lindley suddenly reached for his tranquillizers and the British lads gulped on their orange juices, the American Press lads leaned over to Pat Eddery and started asking him what were the names of the last few horses. Lester started laughing and I was creased up so much that I got cramp – I had to dash to the cloakroom and hang from the coat rail to straighten myself out. When I came back I just had to go up and tell the guy: "I think you have just read out the whole telex!"' The following day the same man also credited Lester with riding three Grand National winners.

Lester had a rather persistent lady admirer who was always turning up to see him when he rode at York. Mike Watt said: 'We were always pulling Lester's leg that she was after his body. He was always on the look out for her, ready to dodge behind anything and anyone to avoid her.

'I was doing the driving from the hotel to the track on this particular day when Lester told me to drive right up to the front rather than go to the car park. "What's up?" I asked him. "It's that woman, I'm sure she's around somewhere," he said before dashing off to the jockeys' room to hide. He also told me not to wait for him on the steps of the weighing room, but to go inside – just in case she was lurking somewhere.

'I parked the car and went into the racecourse – I usually try to get on with some other business on the track so it's not really a social occasion for me and this day was no different. A little later I went to the weighing room to have a word with Lester but there was no sign of him. After a minute his head slowly appeared from behind a pillar and he gestured for me to nip over to see him. Almost at the same time from behind me came this loud screech and the woman Lester had been trying to hide from came rushing past me and right up to him. "There you are Lester, you've been bad to old Dolly haven't you? Trying to hide, but you can't get away from me."

'I suppose some people might think it strange to have nerves of steel for one job yet sometimes turn and run in another situation. Give Lester his due though, he would always sign autographs for his fans and would never leave a young child disappointed. Many times I've seen him sign every book and piece of paper that has been put in front of him. There was a surprising thing about Lester as a rider. Despite all his success over all those years I think he always underestimated the effect that his riding had on people.'

Once in Ireland Lester and Mike Watt were flying to a destination where there was only a grass landing-strip and not a very long one. As they dropped down, the pilot turned round and said it was a trifle misty and there was no way he wanted to take the plane down there because he knew there was a rather large ditch at the end of the runway.

Lester looked down out of the window and said to the pilot: 'Of course you can do it; go on, you can do it.' The pilot wasn't having anything of it though, and Lester had to get tough with him, in the end forcing him to land. The plane straightened up ready for landing – probably it was a white-knuckle job for the pilot – and they came down through the mist, bumped a few times and finally landed. Lester was first out of the plane. He casually walked up to the front of the aircraft to survey its position, followed closely by the pilot whose nerves were in shreds. The plane was literally two feet from the ditch. Lester turned to him and smiled: 'Told you you could do it,' he said walking away with his hands in his pockets.

Lester had never before given the Englishmen abroad so much pleasure as he did when winning the 1969 Washington International at Laurel Park, Maryland, aboard Karabas, trained by the late Bernard van Cutsem at Newmarket. English racing fans had been taunted by their American friends after the previous year's race when the US Press called Lester a 'bum' even though he had won that event on the mighty Sir Ivor.

In 1968 Lester had held up Sir Ivor in order for the colt to see out the one and a half miles on soft ground and preserve his late burst of speed until the optimum moment. This he did exactly and Lester swooped at the last minute to steal the race. The American commentators were far from impressed, however, and began their jibes saying that Sir Ivor should have been ridden differently and that Lester was a handicap to the great horse. Obviously this upset Lester very much and he was determined to make his critics eat their words. So too were Lester's admirers who lived in the States and who had been infuriated to see his reputation sullied.

Come Karabas's turn and Lester was supremely confident he would win. He walked the course and found that the turf – so often hard, pitted and rutted late in the season – was in perfect condition. He even expressed his confidence openly with the Karabas connections and told them there was nothing to worry about. Before the race Lester was in good form, laughing and joking with friends as if he hadn't a care in the world. At the off, Lester had Karabas in a good position tracking the leaders and on the rail. He saw his chance entering the straight where the favourite Hawaii had come off the rails, allowing a gap just big enough for Lester to send Karabas steaming through.

Hitting the front in the short straight, Lester kept Karabas up to his work and the combination went on to win by one and a half lengths. After trotting back to the winner's circle and dismounting with a wide grin, Lester was approached by a posse of pressmen all anxious to hear just how the race had gone.

Again, that familiar question was asked: 'Just when did you think you had the race won, Mr Piggott?'

'Oh, about three weeks ago,' Lester replied.

LESTER'S LAMENT

by JULIE CECIL

Poor old Lester is so short of readies,
Inflation he tries hard to beat;
He's working the children and selling the car
In an effort to make both ends meet.

    Life is so tough for a jockey,
    His diet and expenses are such
    That Sue's housekeeping money goes nowhere,
    As whalemeat costs so bloody much.

You cannot make much of a profit
On a mere twenty thousand a year,
When you've ridden just three thousand winners
In the whole of your thankless career!

    The Queen and Prince Philip felt pity,
    To Ian Balding her trainer she said:
    "My husband and I must sack Waldron
    And finance dear Piggott instead."

Imagine Her Majesty's feelings
When round to the Palace he sent
A request for expenses, a knighthood,
Place money and fifteen percent!

    But life is so tough for a jockey,
    He cannot exist on fresh air;
    He can't feed the wife and the children
    On five Classic winners a year.

But don't worry Lester we'll help you,
We won't see you starve – never that!
Charles St George says that he'll grind the organ
While I'll personally pass round the hat.

    Henry'll dress up as a monkey,
    J. Hindley will don a bear's-skin;
    Ben Hanbury will just be himself and
    We'll see how the money rolls in!!!

CHRISTMAS, 1974